COMPENSATION
CRAZY:

DO WE BLAME AND CLAIM TOO MUCH?

Institute of Ideas
Expanding the Boundaries of Public Debate

COMPENSATION CRAZY:

DO WE BLAME AND CLAIM TOO MUCH?

Institute of Ideas
Expanding the Boundaries of Public Debate

Ellie Lee
John Peysner
Tracey Brown
Ian Walker
Daniel Lloyd

Hodder & Stoughton
A MEMBER OF THE HODDER HEADLINE GROUP

DEBATING MATTERS

Orders: please contact Bookpoint Ltd, 130 Milton Park, Abingdon, Oxon OX14
4SB. Telephone: (44) 01235 827720. Fax: (44) 01235 400454.
Lines are open from 9.00 - 6.00, Monday to Saturday, with a 24 hour message
answering service. Email address: orders@bookpoint.co.uk

British Library Cataloguing in Publication Data
A catalogue record for this title is available from
the British Library

ISBN 0 340 84839 1

First Published 2002
Impression number   10 9 8 7 6 5 4 3 2 1
Year   2007 2006 2005 2004 2003 2002

Copyright © 2002 Hodder & Stoughton

Typeset by Transet Limited, Coventry, England.
Printed in Great Britain for Hodder & Stoughton Educational, a division of
Hodder Headline Plc, 338 Euston Road, London NW1 3BH by Cox & Wyman,
Reading, Berks.

DEBATING MATTERS

CONTENTS

DEBATING MATTERS

 **PREFACE**

Since the summer of 2000, the Institute of Ideas (IOI) has organized a wide range of live debates, conferences and salons on issues of the day. The success of these events indicates a thirst for intelligent debate that goes beyond the headline or the sound-bite. The IOI was delighted to be approached by Hodder & Stoughton, with a proposal for a set of books modelled on this kind of debate. The *Debating Matters* series is the result and reflects the Institute's commitment to opening up discussions on issues which are often talked about in the public realm, but rarely interrogated outside academia, government committee or specialist milieu. Each book comprises a set of essays, which address one of four themes: law, science, society and the arts and media.

Our aim is to avoid approaching questions in too black and white a way. Instead, in each book, essayists will give voice to the various sides of the debate on contentious contemporary issues, in a readable style. Sometimes approaches will overlap, but from different perspectives and some contributors may not take a 'for or against' stance, but simply present the evidence dispassionately.

Debating Matters dwells on key issues that have emerged as concerns over the last few years, but which represent more than short-lived fads. For example, anxieties about the problem of 'designer babies', discussed in one book in this series, have risen over the past decade. But further scientific developments in reproductive technology, accompanied by a widespread cultural distrust of the implications of these developments, means the debate about 'designer babies' is set to continue. Similarly, preoccupations with the weather may hit the news at times of flooding or extreme weather conditions, but the underlying concern about global warming and the idea that man's intervention into nature is causing the world harm, addressed in another book in the *Debating Matters* series, is an enduring theme in contemporary culture.

At the heart of the series is the recognition that in today's culture, debate is too frequently sidelined. So-called political correctness has ruled out too many issues as inappropriate for debate. The oft noted 'dumbing down' of culture and education has taken its toll on intelligent and challenging public discussion. In the House of Commons, and in politics more generally, exchanges of views are downgraded in favour of consensus and arguments over matters of principle are a rarity. In our universities, current relativist orthodoxy celebrates all views as equal as though there are no arguments to win. Whatever the cause, many in academia bemoan the loss of the vibrant contestation and robust refutation of ideas in seminars, lecture halls and research papers. Trends in the media have led to more 'reality TV', than TV debates about real issues and newspapers favour the personal column rather than the extended polemical essay. All these trends and more have had a chilling effect on debate.

But for society in general, and for individuals within it, the need for a robust intellectual approach to major issues of our day is essential. The *Debating Matters* series is one contribution to encouraging contest about ideas, so vital if we are to understand the world and play a part in shaping its future. You may not agree with all the essays in the *Debating Matters* series and you may not find all your questions answered or all your intellectual curiosity sated, but we hope you will find the essays stimulating, thought provoking and a spur to carrying on the debate long after you have closed the book.

Claire Fox, Director, Institute of Ideas

NOTES ON THE CONTRIBUTORS

Tracey Brown is a risk analyst who has worked with a range of companies and institutions faced with an increased risk of litigation, to promote open communication and strategic management. She is the coordinator of the Litigious Society project and author of many articles and papers discussing the rise of litigation in the UK. She has been a vocal critic on television and radio of the growing trend towards litigation avoidance and defensive practices within organizations.

Ellie Lee teaches sociology and social policy at the University of Southampton. Her research interests lie in the areas of the sociology of social problems and policy developments in the areas of the regulation of reproductive technology and mental health. She is commissioning editor for the law section of the *Debating Matters* series.

Daniel Lloyd qualified as a barrister in 1996. After completing pupillage at Cloisters he worked for the law firm Freshfields. He now works in-house for a large communications company. Daniel has taught public law at University College, London, and has published widely on a range of legal issues from a civil liberties perspective. He is currently organizing a conference on the impact of the Human Rights Act on behalf of the campaign group, Freedom and Law.

John Peysner is a solicitor and Professor of Civil Litigation at Nottingham Law School, Nottingham Trent University. He is a newly appointed member of the statutory Civil Justice Council, established to oversee the civil court system. He has worked in private practice, in not-for-profit community law centres and for the last ten years he has researched and taught solicitors how to be more skilful and efficient litigators. This gives him an insider's and outsider's perspective on the so called 'litigation crisis'.

Ian Walker is a Senior Partner in the personal injury department of the law firm Russell Jones & Walker and head of the firm's Maximum Severity Injury Litigation Unit. He specializes in claimant personal injury litigation of all types, including disaster and multiparty cases. Ian is a former President of the Association of Personal Injury Lawyers and is a Senior Fellow of the College of Personal Injury Law. Ian regularly contributes to national press and broadcast on personal injury matters and is former editor-in-chief of the *Journal of Personal Injury Litigation.*

INTRODUCTION
Ellie Lee

On 7 July 2001 Bradford, a city in the north of the UK, witnessed a night of rioting on its streets. According to media reports police, unable to calm the unrest, were pelted with stones, bricks and petrol bombs leaving more than 260 officers injured. By August a claim had been lodged by some police personnel involved for compensation for trauma they allegedly suffered as a result of the events in Bradford. Backed by the Police Federation, claimants, it was reported, could win thousands of pounds if they could prove that Chief Constable Graham Moore neglected his duty of care to the police officers present on that July night. In the same month this claim for compensation made the news, another putative compensation claim was extensively discussed in the media. It was reported that a multimillion pound lawsuit against major airlines was to be launched on behalf of British airline users, said to be suffering from 'Economy Class Syndrome'. According to the *Observer* newspaper, lawyers acting for families whose relatives had died from deep vein thrombosis believed they had an 'extremely strong' case for massive compensation payments to be made. Airlines apparently faced a bill of more than £10 million, for acting negligently in failing to warn UK travellers about the alleged link between air travel and blood clots.

Media coverage of these cases indicates that claiming compensation has emerged as a significant issue of public interest. Cases where it is claimed that institutions or businesses have acted negligently and failed in their duty of care to their clients or employees regularly make the news. (Duty of care is explained later in this Introduction.) And, over the past two years, such cases have become the subject of extensive debate in the press, where the question of whether it is right to 'blame and claim' is a controversial one. This is especially the case when the end result is, or could be, the award of a substantial amount of money in damages as a result of litigation.

The term 'the compensation culture' is used frequently in debate about such litigation. But this term is not a neutral one. It is not used simply as a description of a society where people are able to seek compensation. Rather, where the idea that we live in a 'compensation culture' is invoked, the implication is that the decision to seek compensation, or the award of damages following litigation, is problematic. 'Compensation culture' is, therefore, a pejorative term and often the explanation given for why claims are brought suggests we should be critical of those who 'blame and claim'. Greed for example – both on the part of 'ambulance-chasing' lawyers and on the part of claimants themselves – has often been put forward as an explanation of why compensation is sought by many people these days.

But is this representation of the situation accurate? Is it true to say there is a 'compensation culture'? And if there is, are the explanations commonly on offer for why people might 'blame and claim' convincing? It is in response to these questions that this book has been compiled. Those who have written the essays that follow, while holding competing opinions on a range of questions, agree that a key issue is the need to explain why people might seek compensation today. Their aim in contributing to this book is to go beyond a simplified explanation for this phenomenon – for example, as a manifestation of greed. In doing so, they put forward a range of explanations, which bring with them divergent assessments of the issue of compensation claiming today.

John Peysner assesses claim making from the point of view of the majority in society, who need a means through which they can gain resources. For Peysner, the allegation that greedy people are now prepared to sue at the drop of a hat is simply not true. However, there may be an increase in litigation which, he argues, can be considered as an understandable response to the erosion of collective forms of resource provision, such as the welfare state. While this situation may not be ideal, its representation as a 'compensation culture' is problematic. To suggest that this litigation is necessarily a negative development, showing bad faith on the part of litigants and lawyers, is misplaced. Rather, it may be only current means through which those who need to can gain access to resources. A misrepresentation of the situation as a culture of compensation has emerged, argues Peysner, because of the negative image created of litigation by the development of claims management companies. On the back of the collapse of the UK legal aid system, they have promoted their services through crass television adverts and have given litigation a bad name. There are things that need to change, however, suggests this author and in the final section of his essay, he puts forward some proposals for appropriate methods for resolving disputes in the future.

Tracey Brown in some sense takes a similar starting point – the needs of the majority in society. She contends, however, in contrast to Peysner, that from this standpoint, compensation claiming is a serious problem. While it may benefit the individual litigant, it damages the social fabric in significant ways. Brown argues first that there is, undeniably, a litigation boom in Britain. Those cases that make the headlines are only the tip of the iceberg and those who focus only on cases that get to court, to argue that litigation is not extensive in Britain, are hiding the truth. This author argues that the significant development is in out-of court settlements. Only five per cent of compensation claims are settled in court. The rest are resolved outside courtrooms, in what Brown calls the 'quasi-legal world'. When this world is taken into account, the soaring costs of compensation become very evident and can explain why litigation cost the NHS £500 million in 2000, up from just £85 million in 1991. Second, she contends, this expansion in litigation is a problem. The issue for concern is not simply the sums of money involved or the number of cases. Rather, it is a worrying social shift, which has manifested itself in a propensity to blame and claim. For Brown, the major cause of this shift is a dual process of the erosion of trust between people and the development of an individuated, anti-social outlook, on a wide scale. A propensity to look to the law to solve problems both reflects and encourages these trends and should be seen as a very worrying development.

Ian Walker argues, in stark contrast to Brown, that those who suggest there is a 'compensation culture' are in fact blowing things out of all proportion. The cases that form the basis for much media reporting are extreme and caricature the reality of the situation. Writing from the point of view of the victim of accidents or harm, Walker contends that most cases that are brought – including against doctors, for stress and other psychological illnesses, and against education authorities – are entirely reasonable and those that are not do not get to court. Further, argues Walker, insofar as claims are brought and compensation payouts are won, the effect is positive for society. A propensity to sue is symptomatic of a population 'more conscious of our legal and moral rights', and the effect of litigation is to hold employers, big businesses and public services to account.

Daniel Lloyd disagrees with Walker. He argues that there is a 'compensation culture' and that is something we should worry about. Explaining its development from the point of view of the lawyer concerned with how the law should develop and change, he contends that it is developing in a problematic way. The law is acting paternalistically towards the public by undermining personal responsibility. And, in an undemocratic fashion, judges are adopting a policy-making role in their acceptance of new kinds of claims, which has led to an uneven application of the principles of tort law. For Lloyd, the propensity to sue today cannot be understood simply as a reasonable response to unquestionably negligent acts. Rather, many of the claims being brought are unreasonable and represent a negative development on past trends in litigation. In particular, he suggests, the emergence of claims for psychological injury and the development of US-style class actions, are problematic. He considers how the law has expanded to make these kinds of claim possible and argues that something must be done – ultimately by parliament – to restrict the grounds for litigation.

These essays thus present contrasting views on how to assess litigious activity as it exists in Britain today. Differences of opinion in this regard carry with them contrasting opinions about developments in the law that relates to compensation claims. Has the law gone far enough, or too far, in making it possible for certain kinds of claim to be brought (for example, for psychological damage, or as group actions)? Is it still too difficult for individuals to sue or has it been made too easy already? The remainder of this introduction will briefly discuss the relevant part of the law, in order to indicate the key components of the legal framework that form the subject matter for this debate.

TORT LAW

The legal framework in question is a part of tort law, the tort of negligence. This subject is complex and has been discussed extensively by legal scholars and the discussion here has necessarily been simplified in the brief outline which follows.

The law of negligence assumes that members of a society owe one another a duty of care, outside and in addition to contractual liabilities, depending on the principles of proximity and foreseeability. This means that each of us owes a duty of care to those with whom, in the eyes of the law, we have a proximate relationship and where it is reasonably foreseeable that a person could be harmed by our actions or failure to act.

DUTY OF CARE

This concept is essential in determining whether it is proper that the *plaintiff* (the party who accuses another of acting in a negligent manner) should have the loss they claim they have suffered redistributed to the *defendant* (the party accused of acting in a negligent manner). This approach is informed by the assumption that individuals should, in general, bear their misfortunes alone unless there is some good reason for shifting the loss onto someone else (W. Mansell and J. Conaghan, *The Wrongs of Tort*, 1999). In negligence there are three principal elements that determine the existence of a duty of care. These are proximity, reasonable forseeability and fault. For a plaintiff to succeed it is necessary that they establish each of these elements.

Proximity
For a claim to succeed it must be proved that the defendant was in a sufficiently proximate relationship to the plaintiff so that the defendant could reasonably foresee the consequences of his actions to the plaintiff. By way of example of what is meant by a proximate relationship, fellow road users are considered to be in a proximate relationship with one another, as are doctors and their patients. Exactly what constitutes a proximate relationship is decided on a case-by-case basis and has been subject to debate.

Reasonable forseeability

For a defendant to be found liable the plaintiff must show that it was reasonable for the defendant to foresee that his or her actions (or inactions) would cause the plaintiff harm. A key element in determining this question is the degree of proximity between the plaintiff and defendant. This principle has been the subject of much debate as what is and is not reasonably forseeable has been redefined by successive generations of lawyers.

Fault

The plaintiff must prove that the harm caused was the fault of the defendant. This has led to the maxim 'no liability without fault'. Cane has summarized this principle as follows:

> It is just that a person who causes loss or damage to another by his fault should be required to compensate that other; and... It is just that a person who causes loss or damage to another without fault should *not* be required to compensate that other.
>
> (*The Anatomy of Tort Law*, 1997)

These concepts overlap with each other and in practice are always interlinked. If the plaintiff can establish all three elements then his claim will succeed unless the judges decide that there are very good policy reasons not to impose a duty of care on the defendant.

HOW HAS THE DUTY OF CARE DEVELOPED?

Until the 1930s, the principles established in law that could be regarded as the basis for a 'duty of care' were disparate and unconnected. Lord Atkin brought these principles together and codified the essential elements of the 'duty of care' in a case called *Donaghue v Stevenson* in 1932, with his famous neighbourhood principle:

> You must take reasonable care to avoid acts or omissions which you can reasonably foresee and likely to injure your neighbour. Who, then, in law, is my neighbour? The answer seems to be – persons who are so closely and directly affected by my act that I ought reasonably to have them in contemplation as being so affected when I am directing my mind to the acts or omissions which are called into question.

Thus a duty of care to one's neighbour was established in law. But what is meant by 'reasonably foreseeable' became subject to debate and the vagueness of Lord Atkin's approach allowed many differing interpretations of the neighbourhood principle to emerge.

In 1978 Lord Wilberforce, in a case called *Anns v Merton LBC*, created a two-stage test that came to be known as the Wilberforce test. His two-stage test is as follows. First, if there is, between the defendant and the plaintiff, a sufficient relationship of proximity such that in the reasonable contemplation of the former carelessness on his or her part may be likely to cause damage to the latter, then a *prima facie* duty of care arises. Second, if the first question is answered affirmatively, it is necessary to consider whether there are any policy considerations which ought to negate, or to reduce or limit the scope of the duty or the class of person to whom it is owed, or the damages to which a breach of it may give rise.

This 'two-stage' test, because of its emphasis on *prima facie* duties, was subsequently criticized, since it was thought it would lead to a massive expansion in areas where cases could be brought. Lord Wilberforce's general principle, that a duty of care applies as long as there is proximity, was called into question by a series of judgements from the early 1980s onwards.

As a result of these cases, the law of negligence developed a 'three-stage test', which involves the criteria of reasonable forseeability, proximity and whether it is 'fair, just and reasonable' to impose a duty of care. The aim of this approach was to enable judges to push back or reign in a massive expansion in the tort of negligence, that it was considered earlier approaches would lead to. Whether this project has succeeded or failed forms a major point of disagreement for contributors to this book.

A CHANGING LEGAL LANDSCAPE

The way in which the legal concepts of negligence and fault, harm, proximity, reasonable forseeability and what is just and fair have been defined and applied has changed over time as new cases have been brought. In different areas of life, for example employment, medical practice or education, new legal cases come to set precedents about how these concepts might be interpreted.

It has been argued that the key feature that distinguishes the interpretation of the tort of negligence today from the past is the areas of life and kinds of experiences that are now considered appropriate for interpretation through the prism of liability. As one legal scholar Stapleton has put it: 'We are now seeing whole new types of claims which were simply not considered by practitioners twenty or thirty years ago' ('In Restraint of Tort', in P. Birks (ed.) *The Frontiers of Liability*, 1994). This view is supported by the relatively recent emergence of claims against local authorities and education authorities, relating to the alleged neglect of duty of care in decisions about adoption, medical discharge, exclusion from school and so on, areas previously thought to be covered by the defined statutory duties of the authorities concerned. Compensation claims for damage to psychological well-being, can also be considered a development of this kind. (The psychiatric condition post-traumatic stress disorder, on which many such claims rest, was not defined until 1981 in the USA, and conditions such as stress and lowered self-esteem, which have been used as the basis for legal claims, have even more recently come into use in medical practice.)

Another alleged difference with the past is the emergence of legal action taken by groups of people, for example, that to be taken by British airline users. This innovation was described in the early 1990s as 'one of the most remarkable features of the last decade' (see Frank Furedi, *Complaining Britain*, 1999). It is argued it has become easier for this kind of case to be brought, since restrictions on the right of lawyers to advertise for clients have been loosened. Legal firms can thus, through advertising, encourage the formation of groups of clients and take action on their behalf.

Discussion of these developments poses a range of questions: To what extent has the scope of negligence expanded? If an expansion has taken place, is this development to the advantage of society? Should the law be interpreted in a way that makes it easy or difficult to bring cases? Should it aim to enable claims to be made and continue in its current trajectory? Will this increase social justice and accountability and enable individuals to get only what they rightly deserve? Or does it constitute a misuse of public money, undermine trust and erode individual and social responsibility?

Contributions in the essays that follow provide competing answers to these questions, which we hope will enable readers to consider their own views about these questions and draw some conclusions about whether we do blame and claim too much.

Essay One

COMPENSATION CRAZY: DO WE BLAME AND CLAIM TOO MUCH?

John Peysner

Open your newspaper on virtually any day and you will see headlines such as:

> Don Schell was taking a Prozac-type antidepressant when he killed his wife, daughter and granddaughter, then turned the gun on himself. His son-in-law sued the drug company and won $6.4m.
>
> *The Guardian*

> Here the heat is always on. The US has some of the harshest regulators any company will encounter. They're called lawyers.
>
> *The Observer*

> Who pays for our bad luck as we become more litigious?
>
> *The Times*

> [Of the Bristol Heart Enquiry] There's no incentive to admit error, only to cover up.
>
> *The Guardian*

If we accept current 'informed opinion' it seems that the county is engulfed in a rising tide of litigation where the traditional British stiff upper lip is replaced by a culture of whining, complaining and suing on the American model where the only winners are lawyers. In Bradford, police sue for post-riot stress and school trips are cancelled as teachers fear being sued: where will it all lead? The title of this book raises two questions: Are we compensation crazy? And do we blame and claim too much? I am going to reverse the order of these questions and examine first whether the trend is for an increase in litigiousness and second whether this is a crazy or rational activity for our society, which benefits from the apparent increase in litigation and which benefits from criticizing it.

ARE CLAIMS INCREASING?

This is a simple question with no easy answer. To understand what is happening it is necessary to break down the various steps in bringing a claim. The average citizen may be involved in a wide variety of claims (I exclude family and child cases that excite different concerns). These claims can relate to personal injuries at home, at work or on the road; sex or race discrimination; unfair dismissal; educational provision or a myriad of claims arising out of breaches of contract to provide goods or services. Current surveys suggest that despite the allegation that individuals now sue at the drop of a hat, the usual response to minor injuries, slights at work or defective cars is to do nothing or to complain and if they cannot obtain redress to 'lump it'. If they do decide to take matters further people may contact a lawyer or, in the field of personal injury claims, their first port of call is likely to be a claims management company or claims referral system – of which more later. Once the claim is in the hands of a representative then the potential defendant – insurance company, local authority or employer – is approached with a view to a negotiated settlement. The current court system obliges the parties to exchange information with a view to making a settlement before they start court proceedings. This produces the odd situation that claims, particularly for personal injury, may be increasing but the number of court cases has rapidly fallen. I say 'may be increasing' because, as we will see, litigation is being increasingly commercialized by a reduction in publicly accountable legal aid and by transfer from the open court arena to behind closed doors settlement. In this way data on claims are being driven underground and cloaked in commercial confidentiality.

What then is the real activity in this sector? The ultimate players such as the motor insurers, the employer liability insurers and the NHS are reporting rising levels of claims and many insurers claim that their business is unprofitable. It is quite possible that the *level* of individual claims is going up. Certainly in the NHS, claimants are now represented by highly specialized solicitors who may reject weak claims but who will be able to ensure that the damages in successful cases include all possible claims. Another example is the murky area of credit hire. In former times, if your car was off the road after an accident the bus was often the only alternative. Nowadays, many garages are linked to credit hire companies that provide a 'free' service of a loan car on the basis that the charges are rolled up into the main claim. Sometimes this can cause difficulty as the other driver's insurance company may be prepared to pay for a driver's personal injuries but not the whole of the car hire. However, in many cases such hire is paid with the result that the average claim is higher.

It is important to be careful about taking criticism of the 'claims culture' at face value. Insurance is a form of gambling. If insurers have historically miscalculated their 'book' by charging premiums at too low a rate (perhaps to bring in business) they may find it convenient to complain about excessive litigiousness in order to find an excuse for an overall increase in premium levels.

While the position is unclear let us assume, for the purpose of the argument, that British people are becoming more litigious. In passing, we should not assume that this means we are aping the USA.

Historically, although there have been more claims in the USA than in Britain, our nearer neighbours in Germany have long had much higher levels of litigation than us. The next question is why are growing numbers of claims such a problem?

IS SEEKING REDRESS A BAD THING?

Our society has increasingly moved from the post-war consensus on collective provision to individual provision and the individual 'rights' that flow from these new arrangements. Workers who do not belong to trade unions will seek to rely on rights against dismissal enforced through tribunals. New rights not to be discriminated against on the grounds of race, sex, gender, sexual orientation and disability are coordinated by central bodies, but much of the challenge to bad behaviour will be dependent on individuals bringing cases. If you are missold a pension you are likely to seek help from the ombudsman but also explore the possibility of a claim in the courts. If your child is refused a school place or special provision a tribunal may be the only avenue for redress. I make no great claim for these rights at their current stage of development and, in fact, disputes about them rarely lead to litigation, but they may well be the only means of seeking a remedy in a society that has moved away from the concept that the state and the local authority provide for all.

This wider concept of litigiousness has in fact been neglected in the media by a concentration on a relatively small area of litigation: claims for personal injury. No one talks about the growth over the last few decades in commercial claims between corporations, international trade claims and intellectual property litigation. This is not a cause for concern: indeed the Government is trying to promote the London courts as a world centre for dispute resolution. What exercises the mind of media commentators and the chattering classes is the 'threat' to our social structure from people suing after they have had a rail accident, a road accident, an accident at work, when they have tripped on a pavement or been damaged by a pharmaceutical product. While I can see that for soldiers to claim against the MOD for battlefield injuries may seem bizarre, if they could have been better protected by the exercise of foresight, then compensation seems appropriate. While school trips may be less exciting, if teachers are constrained from taking kids out to sea with inadequate training or proper life jackets, then shouldn't we ask grieving parents if they would have preferred better precautions? To understand the present situation we must set it into its context. How has the compensation system developed?

THE DEATH OF LEGAL AID

The shift from collective to individual provision has become the guiding principle of all mainstream political parties reflected in the trend to reduce public expenditure. While some elements, such as social security payments, have stubbornly resisted any major cuts, governments – both Tory and Labour – casting their eye around for easier targets have alighted on the legal aid budget. The British legal aid scheme, established in 1948, involved a complex interaction between individuals bringing or defending claims whose cases were submitted by their lawyers for support by an authority funded by the government. Individuals faced a means test and their cases were subjected to a relatively benign assessment to see if it was reasonable for them to be advanced. The lawyers then charged the authority for their work or if they were successful their costs would be wholly or partly recoverable from the losing party. The need for the scheme was based on the fact that lawyers have always been as expensive as emergency plumbers on an hourly basis and, usually, their 'repairs' take longer. Legal expense insurance – insuring in advance against the possibility of having to pay your own lawyer and the opponent's lawyer if you lose – while popular in Germany has, so far, failed to take off in the UK.

In fact, much of legal aid, such as personal injury cases, did not turn out to be a burden on the treasury as recovered costs matched the expenditure by the lawyers; in effect the client borrowed legal aid money to keep the lawyer ticking over with instalment payments and at the end of the case there was a final balancing act. What worried governments were not straightforward personal injury cases but more complex areas such as medical negligence, judicial review of public decisions and drug cases involving large numbers of claims, where lawyers' bills were escalating.

Government response was to slowly strangle legal aid provision by reducing the number of people who were eligible. Eventually, most earners and even people on high benefits could not obtain legal aid and yet the rump of cases seemed to cost more and more. Looking forward, policy makers saw that the potential for increasing assertiveness by citizens would lead to more expenditure. What could be done to provide people with access to legal help without costing public money? The answer was to shift the risk from the state to lawyers and a new breed of after-the-event insurers.

CLAIMS MANAGEMENT COMPANIES AND THE LITIGATION CRISIS

THE NEW SCHEME

How could legal aid be replaced without removing access to the courts for the ordinary citizen? This question puzzled administrations since the 1980s and, in the context of the panic over an emerging 'compensation culture', it must not be forgotten that all governments recognize that access to the courts is a basic human right. The problem is that, for most people, effective access requires lawyers and lawyers cost money. How could this circle be squared? Legal expense insurance remained a hard sell. While people can imagine their house burning down, they find it hard to galvanize their chequebooks towards purchasing cover for what seems to be a remote risk of being sued or suing (at present the legal expense insurers are involved in a marketing charge, bundling up their products cheaply with other types of cover). In the USA, the problem is solved for personal injury, and some employment and discrimination cases, by a system of contingency fees. These involve the lawyer being given a cut of the damages if the case is won and nothing if it is lost. The system works well for two reasons: damages are higher so the client still retains a reasonable amount and, unlike the British system, the loser does not pay the winner's legal fees.

The first attempt at legal aid replacement therapy was the standard conditional fee. In this scheme the lawyer charges nothing if the case is lost but gets an additional reward of up to 100 per cent of costs if the case is won. This is good news for the skilful risk-taking lawyer – the winning cases should make up for any losing ones – but not so great for the client. If the client wins, then the damages are reduced by the lawyer's reward and if the client loses then there are no damages *and* the client has to pay the winner's costs.

This system languished until the New Labour Government introduced a wave of changes that have transformed the legal scene and form the background to the 'compensation crisis'. First, legal aid for personal injury work was effectively abolished, creating demand for a new way of financing cases. Second, 'after-the-event' insurance was introduced

8

to cover the cost of the opponent's costs if a case was lost. (This insurance can also be used for non-conditional fee cases where the loser has to pay the opponent's costs *and* his own. Here the lawyer trades less risk for less reward.) Third, and most controversially, the 'after-the-event' insurance premium and the lawyer's additional reward in a conditional fee case became recoverable from the loser *as well as* normal costs. Essentially, a system has been created where the client takes no risk and the additional costs of the risk-taking lawyer and 'after-the-event' insurer falls on defendants: mostly motor and employer's liability insurers, who recycle the risk to their customers through increasing premiums.

ENTER THE CLAIMS MANAGEMENT COMPANIES

There is no doubt that the Government regarded its new scheme as a simple replacement for legal aid at the then current levels of activity and thought it would simply allow solicitors to carry on offering a service to their existing legal aid clients, with a modest increase to accommodate those who had lost their legal aid eligibility. Abolishing legal aid for personal injury cases carries the benefit that most of these cases are successful. (Despite the views of some commentators, most personal injury claimants are honest and do not make up their injuries. The law is meant to protect them against carelessness by motorists, authorities who fail to mend pavements and bad employers, so they should win most of their cases.) Once the system had bedded down for personal injury cases, it could be extended to replace other areas of legal aid, such as employment and consumer cases. However, once the genie was out of the bottle marked 'legal market capitalism', a wave of non-lawyer entrepreneurs entered the game with a new business model: the claims management company.

Claims Direct and dozens of clones operate a simple system. They trawl for accident cases by advertising or direct marketing, administer the cases and then farm them out to a tied panel of solicitors. The companies earn their money by opaque and fiendishly complex systems of referral fees and charges, but the result is that their marketing and add-on costs create an additional burden on the defendant insurers, who face having to pick them up on top of normal lawyer costs. While there are other business models, such as National Accident Helpline, that are simply marketing and referral systems, it is the claims management companies and their factoring businesses which have made the biggest impact.

CRASS ADVERTS AND BAD PUBLICITY

If the changes consequent on abolishing legal aid had been hidden behind the cosy and conventional façade of solicitors' offices then, in my view, there would have been little of the current media concern about the 'compensation crisis'. Costs paid by motor insurers might well have gone up with some increase in premiums but business would have gone on pretty much as normal. What changed things was a campaign for new business by the claims management companies behind a vanguard of unprecedented hard sell advertising for legal business that tarred lawyers (not always the public's most favourite group) with the tactics of businesses which they did not own or control.

These advertisements dominate daytime television and they repay attention by any student of the mores of marketing in the postmodern age. Most of the early campaigns were heavily influenced by legal advertising in the USA and were very much 'in your face'. In my view the nadir was reached by one early offering. A glamorous young woman looks longingly at a sports car and says: 'I've always wanted one of those and now I have had an accident I can have one.' A soothing voice then introduces the slogan 'Every cloud has a silver lining'. This approach is entirely inappropriate to personal injury cases where damages are very limited and simply aimed at putting clients back in the position they would have been in had they not suffered the wrong. Such advertising suggests that litigation is a game rather than an attempt to offer some redress to an injured person.

The constant repetition of such a crass approach in all media generated an enormous puff of publicity and moral panic among commentators who were suggesting that the country was about to be engulfed in a wave of claims. While the *Daily Mail*, *The Sun* and Simon Jenkins in *The Times* (strange bedfellows these) had a wider focus, that took in concerns about burglars suing house owners who assaulted them and policeman claiming for post-traumatic stress, it was the claims management companies that created open season on 'grasping' lawyers and 'greedy' clients.

The denouement was not long in coming in the shape of the formidable consumer pundit Anne Robinson and the crusading programme *Watchdog*. She targeted the then market leader, Claims Direct, alleging that it was failing to ensure, in all cases, that its clients retained a fair share of money recovered by their lawyers. Too much seemed to be sticking to the hands of the claims management company. The rights and wrongs of the argument are too complex to discuss here but the result was catastrophic for Claims Direct's share price and it has never really recovered. On a wider basis the whole market was adversely affected and it has responded by reorganizing and toning down its approach. Recent advertising stresses service elements, an introduction by the company to a specialist solicitor; or simply uses mood music with virtually no reference to making a claim to obtain damages. One example is introduced with a downbeat feeling, with a wintry dark scene moving on to sunlit uplands as the mood lifts to welcome a successful settlement. Sports cars and greed are nowhere to be seen.

COMMENTATORS AND THE LITIGATION CRISIS

Whoever started the media backlash against the 'compensation crisis', there is no doubt that commentators jumped in with both feet. It will now be very difficult to conduct a sensible debate about the rights and wrongs of seeking redress. It seems now to be a law of nature that we are about to be overwhelmed by an American style 'compensation culture'. This approach makes the natural but quite mistaken assumption that our legal, social and political system is simply a pale copy of the USA. In fact, in matters of law and litigation we are very different: both in process and in outcomes. The USA imported its legal system from eighteenth-century England complete with sheriffs, bail bondsmen and juries. Because they did not trust centralized forms of government they elected virtually every office holder, particularly judges in the state system. They still cling to this model of representative democracy, electing numerous minor officials including county probate commissioners and other functionaries. While they may want to elect their judges, they do not trust them and so while we abolished juries in civil trials, leaving the decisions to professional judges, they retained them. The result is that many trials, in particular personal injury cases, are conducted before juries who retain a healthy scepticism about large corporations and particular drug, oil and chemical companies and are well aware that the claimant's personal injury case will be funded under the contingency fee system with the lawyer taking up to one-third of the damages. Juries take this into account and adjust their awards upwards to ensure that the injured party is left with sufficient damages.

The Hollywood films *A Civil Action* and *Erin Brockovich* offer reasonably accurate portrayals of how this system works. High awards are sometimes made by a jury to punish a company for bad behaviour, an approach not available in the UK. In turn this leads to propaganda from the corporate lobby attacking the 'fat cat' personal injury lawyers in an attempt to influence public opinion, the public from which future juries will be drawn. The most notorious example of this is the 'McDonald's Coffee Cup Case' that was presented by the defendant lobby as a ludicrously high award for a relatively minor injury. In fact, the claimant suffered third-degree burns and it appears that the jury made a high award, substantially reduced later, because they thought the company should have settled rather than let the case go to trial. This approach, which in turn increases the general level of settlement awards, can produce spectacularly high and unpredictable levels of damages. In England, we do things very differently. Our awards are broadly laid down in guidelines set by the judges and they are far from generous. While we may be moving into a period where the frequency of claims increases we will not see US-style spectacularly high damages.

The problem is that the commentators who comment adversely have identified problems in the 'cure', when they should have been concentrating on the 'disease'. The need is to identify appropriate methods of resolving disputes, which will vary, and to seek efficient ways of delivering access to advice and representation to the public. I hold no brief for legal cases that recover limited damages that are far outweighed by the legal costs involved. Cost benefit analysis should be applied to the whole industry of litigation but this does not imply that problems of the *process* mean that the *right* to claim should be eliminated. The question must be asked what option, other than litigation, is available. What is needed is an examination of the whole area and a new prescription to temper justice with economy. The option to have rights without remedies is a recipe for making rights irrelevant in the modern world.

A NEW PRESCRIPTION

It follows that the question 'Do we blame and claim too much' needs to be addressed in different contexts. I suggest the following divisions as a basis for this examination; cases against the state, disaster cases, cases against the NHS and cases against insurers. These areas overlap and the partition is to an extent arbitrary but to do otherwise risks limiting appropriate methods of redress in some areas because of problems, real or perceived, in others.

THE CITIZEN AND THE STATE

The increasing number of cases brought against the national government and other organs of the state, such as schools, local government, social security authorities, the police and so on, is a relatively recent phenomenon. It has been fuelled by developments in public law that require authorities to act fairly. To this has been added the introduction into UK domestic law of the concept of human rights as an essential civil right of the citizen along with the right not to be discriminated on grounds of gender, disability or ethnic origin. This area is developing apace and cases are testing the limits of these rights. Questions being asked through these cases are: Is there a right to privacy? Should a settled relationship be equated in legal terms with marriage? Has an interest group the right to take action to protect the environment?

In terms of the argument over excessive litigation, the main feature of these types of case is that they are difficult to win, legally complex and do not necessarily produce any compensation at all or only limited damages. For this reason, they are unsuitable for a conditional fee approach and will remain funded by legal aid or interest groups. They can be, however, very expensive in legal costs and are unlikely to be covered by legal expense insurance or after-the-event insurance. At the same time many of these problems have cheaper dispute resolution arrangements through ombudsmen or tribunals such as those dealing with educational needs or social security. All this suggests that the growth of litigation in this area will be constrained. Even so the challenge to critics who wish to curtail activity by lawyers in this area is to ask: What is the alternative? It is fundamental to our human and civic rights that authority be kept in check. Those who argue otherwise should ask whether organs of the state such as the police could safely be left to protect the rights of citizens with no prospect of their actions being tested in the courts.

THE CITIZEN AND DISASTERS

A limited but high-profile area of litigation has been that related to disasters. These come in two types: 'instant' (a single incident such as a rail crash or a building blowing up) and 'creeping' such as the HIV litigation against the blood transfusion authorities or mass pharmaceutical cases. The former are less problematic and are often associated with, or prompt, the authorities to set up enquiries that lead to improved safety. One does not have to be overly paranoid to believe that curbing the ability of citizens to litigate against privatized railway companies would do nothing to encourage better safety standards.

The 'creeping' disasters are more problematic. A litigation response to an allegedly defective drug will involve a mass of cases brought together in a group with a coordinating solicitor and a number of individual firms. Experience has shown that these can be unwieldy and expensive operations which can acquire a life of their own where the legal costs far outweigh the damages and basic issues, such as did the drug cause the symptoms or would they have happened anyway to a patient with this disease, tend to be lost sight of in the mass of detail. Both the Legal Services Commission and the Government are striving towards a more rational system that may curb excesses without preventing claimants bringing cases collectively which as individuals would be impossible to launch.

THE CITIZEN AND THE NHS

The NHS represents the last vestige of the great post-war social welfare settlement still supported by the vast majority of the population and, in principle, by all political parties. As such, litigating against it has some of the unpleasant connotations of litigating within a family. Matters might have been arranged from the start of the scheme so that anyone who emerged from a hospital with a bad result might have been treated in the same way. Whether their result was due to clinical negligence or simply the natural progression of disease in long-term care, adequate income support and appropriate lump sums could have been available for all in difficulties, on an equal basis. In practice this has never been the case. Only those who were able to demonstrate that their outcome was worsened by negligent treatment would receive compensation.

The process of clinical negligence litigation has never been an easy one and it has always been hit and miss. The judges put hurdles in its way out of fear that it would encourage defensive medicine, because legal aid funding was hard to obtain for most wage earners, and the cost of instructing a solicitor on a private basis was prohibitive. Many claimant solicitors dabbled in the field with disastrous results. Often extensive and expensive investigations still left it unclear as to whether negligence caused the bad result or whether it would have happened anyway. However, over the last 20 years, the pace of litigation has quickened and the NHS litigation bill has increased. This has happened as lawyers became more skilled in the field through specialization, as medical experts became less partisan and more available and as the public began to realize that a poor result from medical treatment, in a significant number of cases, was contributed to by a lack of resources and staff negligence.

The current response of the Government is to look to cap damages and discourage litigation. At the same time it aims to encourage 'evidence-based' medicine where sound and tested techniques, rather than the implicit acceptance of health workers' judgement is the guiding light. My own view is that the move towards more rational medicine has only come about because of the threat of litigation and the demonstration through cases, however hit or miss, that certain techniques or individual clinicians were not competent. I hope that the expected changes will maintain the pressure on professionals to offer a good service while keeping costs under control. I remain unconvinced.

THE CITIZEN AND THE INSURERS

The future of the vast mass of compensation cases – largely personal injury against insurers – remains unclear. One possibility is that the claims management companies will colonize the whole sector expanding into related fields such as employment and discrimination cases and employ solicitors rather than refer cases to them. However, their onward expansion may be limited by a recent case that has curtailed the ability of the companies to recover all their administrative costs and to make profit, making their business model less attractive. Another possibility is that the supermarkets will move into this business, as they did with banking and insurance, and use their economies of scale and IT power, to produce a cost effective alternative. I would hope that a service alternative based on skilled legal professionals will still offer a viable alternative, but now the genie is out of this particular bottle and the profits in the system are of interest to the wider business community, I am not sure that lawyers have the wherewithal or vision effectively to compete.

If the claims management companies are restrained then the increase in damages, with more people being legitimately compensated, will be recycled through increased insurance premiums in a more orderly fashion. I cannot find one reason why legitimate motor or accident claims should not be paid. However, the compensation system is not the only way of organizing redress. If the community of motorists underwrite the compensation system for motor accidents through increased insurance premiums perhaps we should introduce 'no fault' schemes on the model of some states in the USA. In these arrangements motorists pay a compulsory levy, which supports a simple system for compensating those injured in accidents without requiring them to prove negligence.

CONCLUSION

Could the no-fault model be extended to cover all accident cases and would it solve the 'compensation crisis'? A 'no fault' scheme to cover all personal injury cases was introduced in New Zealand. The scheme suffered from a particular defect: the claimant still had to prove causation, that is, prove that a medical accident had caused the injury complained of, rather than the natural outcome of the disease. However, there was no requirement to prove negligence either in the area of medical injury, pharmaceutical injury or road injury. The difficulty that has emerged is that such a scheme is extremely vulnerable to the pressure on central government budgets. In the New Zealand case, an incoming administration slashed the scheme's expenditure. As the right of individuals to take action in the courts had been abridged they were left in a much worse situation.

'No-fault' schemes have been raised in the UK from time to time, particularly for clinical negligence. In my view a generalized scheme would either increase costs to such an extent that the scheme would become unviable or the compensation limits would have to be set so low as to be unjust. Our current compensation scheme with all its faults with the recent innovations that have made it more accessible represents a reasonable compromise that requires a constant and informed critique but not a knee-jerk cry that we 'blame and claim too much'.

Essay Two

THE SOCIAL COSTS OF A COMPENSATION CULTURE
Tracey Brown

Do we live in what could be described as a litigious society or, as the press like to call it, a 'compensation culture'? Until very recently British commentators saw a culture of litigation and compensation claiming as a peculiarly American phenomenon. Commentators have long been bemused by the 'ambulance-chasing' culture of the United States and the often curious legal cases and settlements that result. In our perception of an America dominated by the pursuit of redress through the law, we are hardly surprised to discover that they have more lawyers than dentists. By contrast, the British have commonly been depicted as eschewing civil justice in favour of a stiff upper lip in the face of accidents and misfortune that are not of their own making.

When compensation claims have set precedents or made news headlines, they have often been dismissed as exceptional, frivolous and evidence of greedy lawyers importing 'fast buck' schemes from the United States. For Americans, runs the popular wisdom, there is no such thing as an accident – someone can always be held blameworthy under the tort system. In fact, as we will see, the claiming and blaming response to accidents is already deeply embedded within British society but the full extent of this remains unrecognized and is often denied. The expectation that injuries lead to compensation is now widespread and fear of being sued dictates a large range of activities. The fact that there are vehement objections to the cost of compensation payments, whether from *Daily Mail* leader writers or the Department of Health, implies that there is some resistance to a US-style 'sue you' character developing in British public life, but these criticisms are marginal to the way that society is being restructured around litigiousness and litigation avoidance.

A COMPENSATION CULTURE?

From an examination of court statistics, you could be forgiven for thinking that we have not, at least not yet, gone down the American path. Since the early 1990s the number of civil claims heard in the high court (and the county courts) has been falling – from nearly 20,000 in the high court a decade ago to around 4,000 in recent years. Personal injury lawyers and other advocates of increased legal redress argue that the British are still unwilling to demand compensation and need to be made more aware of their rights following an accident. According to a recent estimate in *The Times*, there are three million 'injured people' out there who have yet to benefit from the compensation they are 'due'. Organizations such as the Consumers Association, patients' groups and the Association of Personal Injury Lawyers (APIL) argue that individuals who pursue claims represent only a small percentage (perhaps as little as five per cent) of those who have been wrongfully injured through attributable negligence.

Yet our culture is already full of indicators that Britain *is* in the throes of a compensation culture. There are regular press reports about previously unthinkable claims – by police officers stressed by criminal investigations, drunk patrons tripping on pavements, dinner party guests falling off chairs – as well as reports of 'record payouts' to victims. At the accident and emergency ward of the local hospital, posters and business cards of personal injury law firms and claims brokers are on display, reminding us 'where there's blame, there's a claim'. Daytime television carries many advertisements from the same firms, parading the payouts to a man who fell off a ladder and to a child who had an accident in the playground. More substantial indicators also suggest that there has been a cultural shift in attitudes to blaming and claiming in Britain. Record highs in compensation payouts and legal costs have been announced annually for the past four years by the NHS Litigation Authority, the Medical Defence Union (a mutual fund to cover doctors' legal risks), employers' organizations and the police authorities. And whether a pre-emptive move or simply an overreaction, many British organizations are following their American counterparts in pursuing extensive litigation avoidance strategies. Local authorities are restricting the kind of activities and public spaces on offer; hospitals refuse to admit independent midwives; obstetricians are encountering prohibitive indemnity costs; workplaces have introduced stress counselling; parents are being confronted with waiver forms for more and more of their children's activities. Large companies, medical organizations and local authorities have growing legal departments to handle complaints and claims.

Particular concern has been expressed about the toll of personal injury claims on public services. The Lord Chancellor's Department and the Department of Health have set up working committees to look at protecting the National Health Service from the rising cost of claims by complainants. The costs of clinical negligence action against National Health Service trusts reached over £500 million in 2000, from just £85 million in 1991, which represents a significant diversion of the health service budget away from the provision of healthcare services. Indemnity and claims costs have also increased for the Medical Defence Union (MDU), from £29 million in 1992, to £67 million in 1997.

There is no shortage of concern about the cost of compensation claiming. Politicians have declared that they want to restructure the medical negligence system; the Institute of Directors and the Confederation of British Industry have pointed out the cost to British business of lifting the lid on awards from employment tribunals; the British Medical Association is anxious to reduce the time doctors spend on administration of claims; several senior judges have argued that they need better knowledge of the broader social impact to guide them in the award of compensation; a succession of home secretaries has been lobbied by the police authorities to address the leakage of funds and staff to compensation claims. Yet the figures continue to grow. It appears that the compensation culture is not readily subjected to policy intervention or what some people see as the common sense barriers to its going too far.

THE EXPANSION OF THE QUASI-LEGAL WORLD

The main reason for the disjuncture between the formal appearance of declining legal actions and its apparently runaway costs is that the vast majority of claim making in Britain takes place on the fringes of the legal system. For example, at the same time as the number of negligence claims in the high court has declined, indicators like insurance payments and local authority budgets show that payouts have increased in both quantum (the amount paid out) and frequency. According to the National Health Service Litigation Authority (NHSLA), only three per cent of claims reach court – the vast majority are settled at a much earlier stage. Other estimates have suggested that all negligence claims heard in court represent around five per cent of total claims made and, with the growth in motor accident claims, it is probably now much smaller.

legal world that has grown up in the shadow of the law. This shadow legal world is, however, recognized as appropriate avenues of redress: New Labour's recent and ongoing Access to Justice reforms are very much predicated on these developments.

Although some personal injury lawyers still point to the court statistics to deny any 'compensation culture', it has become more widely recognized now that there is a problem and that most claim-making activity takes place outside the court system, where claims are not subject to full legal scrutiny.

The real importance of the quasi-legal world is not simply that it reveals a far higher level of claims making than is evident in the courts, but it enables a redefinition of the law, which further feeds the 'compensation culture'. Because of its lack of legal scrutiny, the shadow legal world enables greater flexibility in the interpretation of legal principles. For many decades, the allocation of blame in accidents was restricted by established precedent. In a rugby match incident, for example, the plea of *volenti non fit injuria* (plaintiff consents to the risk) would have held firm in the face of compensation claims against referees who did not predict a broken neck before it happened. Now, such boundaries of liability are not reliably applied, when the vast majority of settlements occur outside the courts. The consequence of this is that the organizations on the receiving end of claims are trying to find other ways to avert them because they cannot leave it to legal judgement. Perversely for them, the claims avoidance strategies that they are innovating have the effect of further entrenching a culture built around our potential liability.

And it is here that an important cultural shift is taking place. The expansion of this shadow legal world shows that relationships – between employer and employee, customer and service provider, schools and pupils – are being formalized and conducted with reference to the law as a source of mediation far more extensively than has thus far been acknowledged. It highlights a crisis in the conduct of relationships, where the informal duties and responsibilities between people are becoming more formally defined and enforced in a greater number of instances.

THE EROSION OF INFORMALITY

The emergence and expansion of the quasi-legal world forms part of a broader social and cultural shift. The significance of litigiousness in British society cannot be measured only in terms of the number of people seeking compensation or the amounts paid out. The history of the rise of compensation culture is the history of how we deal with accidents on both a personal and a social level.

It is precisely these less visible effects of growing dependence on legal remedies that are of greatest social significance. Both in-court and out-of-court claiming activity are pushing against any traditional reticence about allocating blame and defining responsibility. It may be true that many people are still unfamiliar with the details of whether and how to make a legal claim – for example they may not be aware that what constitutes negligence in the law is not simply making a mistake. But the way that people behave following an accident suggests that they instinctively feel an entitlement following an accident. I am constantly surprised by the number of people who 'know' that the first thing one does after a rear-impact collision on the roads is complain about a stiff neck. Whiplash injury is difficult to define or dispute and entitles the injured party to personal injury damages.

Attempts to define responsibility, in order that everyone knows where they stand and what their rights are, make our relations more formal. Many areas of social interaction now are being conducted with reference to formalized contracts and duties, often as a way of trying to avoid compensation claims. Organizations' attempts to insulate themselves from compensation claims have been largely unsuccessful (as even the largest international risk consultancy firm admits!). It seems that no amount of risk management in the NHS can turn around the trend of rising claims. No amount of stress counselling in the workplace can prevent employers from finding themselves called to tribunals. On the contrary, the institutionalized accommodations to victims' claims that are the bedrock of these strategies, such as independent review procedures and more extensive consumer compensation schemes, largely serve to encourage their advance. In their efforts to show that they take claims for redress seriously, institutions are helping to spread the vocabulary of compensation and the psychology of personal damage. In fact, our touchy-feely, customer-friendly, client-oriented, victim-sensitive society breeds far more claims for compensation than the bullish, hard nosed business approach ever did!

The problem with this approach is that the more formal relationships become, the more likely it is that people will pursue a case at law rather than sort it out any other way. An indication of this tendency in Britain is the extension of professional liability insurance cover to relationships that were previously rarely the subject of compensation claims. A few of the latest examples include non-professional referees, voluntary trustees and social clubs. Acts between people and between people and organizations that were previously informal, such as attending a football match, coping with office politics or putting up with noisy children next door, are being subjected to legal claims. People in relationships that in the past usually escaped legal enforcement now seek increasing professional intervention in their disputes and, interestingly, they often back up their claims with well-documented records of the other party's activity, demonstrating a developed sense of 'knowing their rights'.

The expansion of legal redress is not solely responsible for people making claims, but acts in concert with wider individualizing trends. In British society, the general ambiguity about authority – whether exercised by businesses, medical professions, schools or government agencies – exists alongside uncertainties about family life and interpersonal relationships. A lack of clarity about what is 'appropriate' behaviour helps to stimulate misunderstanding and conflict; in the context of a litigious climate people are more likely to experience these conflicts as a profound sense of personal injury. They are no longer just slighted or badly treated: the aggrieved person has become injured, offended, victimized, traumatized, damaged and abused. These conditions constitute a potential entitlement for compensation and therefore encourage a profound sense of injury among potential claimants. As people have become accustomed to being suspicious of leaving problems to be resolved informally (whether bullying in the playground or paying for a damaged car after an accident), the extension of the law has become acceptable and even inevitable.

THE EFFECTS OF THE COMPENSATION CULTURE

Some people – particularly personal injury lawyers – think this is a good thing and that what we are seeing is a liability revolution in the name of 'social justice'. It is argued that the threat of legal action, direct or implied, leads to greater corporate responsibility and increased professional care and diligence. The expansion of compensation claiming is believed to contribute to improvements in public services and more clearly defined responsibilities between institutions and individuals.

In fact, we are seeing some very different consequences. The effects of liability are actually counterintuitive. Where we imagine the threat of legal action might be beneficial, opening up powerful institutions to the demands of the powerless, there are quite different outcomes. The effect of litigiousness is to change the way we organize and conduct our relationships and social networks. These changes in behaviour – often caused by fear of litigation and attempts to avoid it – might best be understood as a kind of *litigation consciousness*. In the past few years in Britain there has been an unprecedented expansion of liability. Liability is the means through which litigiousness impinges upon all of us, exposing the skilful surgeon to the same fear of legal action as the reckless one (just as with rules and regulations, diligent professionals appear most affected by fear of litigation). The introduction of a new liability, whether through new precedent or a threat of being sued, forces an anticipation of legal action. It transforms the role of the law of tort from restorative justice into a regulatory system. As a regulator, however, liability is very weak and it is arbitrary as to whom it punishes. If we really think that a practice is dangerous and should be punished, it should surely be dealt with at a broader social and possibly regulatory level.

The possibility of being held legally responsible introduces significant doubt into our conduct and interaction with one another. We imagine the possible legal consequences of what we do, which are not necessarily the same as the social consequences. In a sense it is quite irrelevant whether the 'one-off' case, where the rugby referee was held responsible for a player's injuries, for example, will ever be repeated. Regardless, every rugby referee would now be foolish not to clarify his responsibilities and perhaps think twice about what is, after all, only a leisure activity – even a community service.

The rise in compensation claiming has encouraged a desire to avoid responsibility and therefore liability. For a long period of time, the rail owning company Railtrack refused to remove its Signal 109, despite widespread concerns that it had played a role in the Paddington train crash, because its lawyers suggested that removing it was tantamount to accepting liability. Likewise, saying sorry is no longer a spontaneous response that we can expect from doctors or officials: it needs to be checked with the lawyers first.

We have also experienced a rise in defensive behaviour. There is growing evidence of defensive medicine, which a number of medical specialists now admit to, whereby patients are sent for unnecessary tests to avoid any future risk of litigation. Quite aside from the costs of these, patients are often very worried by what they feel the tests imply – that they may be suffering from various serious conditions. Contemplation of possible legal action also affects other professionals including auditors, accountants, dentists, lawyers, surveyors, architects and so on. Their advice is confused by trying to cover every eventuality and there is a greater emphasis on documenting and form filling on every encounter to cover one's back (rather than because it improves the quality of service).

Far from increasing accountability, the threat of litigation appears to have reduced the amount of openness and information sharing in some areas. Air traffic control incidents used to be recorded and exchanged across the world to pick up any regular patterns. Now the fear of legal action inhibits the process. Likewise, it is not surprising to find that a consequence of several high profile pharmaceutical group actions – which are very lucrative for lawyers – is to reduce the sharing of information in peer-reviewed journals. If you speak to academic clinical specialists, you will find that the majority are aware of the risk that preliminary results and observations can be used in litigation.

It may be that many concerns about the presence of greater litigiousness across society are put aside because people feel that it is good to see big corporations taking a financial hit from unfortunate individuals. A source of this view is the portrayal of compensation culture as a tussle between the big corporate sector, with fat pockets, and the little man (the David to their Goliaths). While relatively few companies have been plunged into 'crisis' by the volume of compensation claims, even here there is arguably a wider price to be paid. We all stand to pay through increased product prices and insurance premiums passed on by sued companies and institutions, as has been widely argued by writers in the United States – where the high levels of compensation are making themselves felt as a 'tax' on society's wealth. However, the more worrying consequences of compensation culture are in the sphere of social amenities, where the volume of cases and the quantum have an impact on resources. A good example of this is the predicament of Manchester City Council, which now spends more on compensating people who fall over on their streets – 'slippers and trippers' – than it does on repairing the roads! A further unintended consequence of increasing litigation risk is the withdrawal of services because the risk of being sued is seen as too high to bear.

Our perception of liability also causes us to have significant doubts about our interaction with one another – significant because it affects the responsibilities we are prepared to take on. We might have these significant doubts about looking after other people's children, for example, or about volunteering to help community projects or youth club outings. This heightened awareness of possible litigation destroys our ability to build relationships based on trust. And it discourages people from taking responsibility for one another and themselves. Perversely, for those seeking increased social responsibility and safety, in societies in which people do not take responsibility for themselves, they do not behave responsibly.

This withdrawal of the willingness to take on responsibility for providing services for others is most keenly felt where children are concerned. It is perhaps surprising that any teachers at all are willing to take children on venture holidays or outings now that even the very small risk of misfortune carries a big price in the almost inevitable consequence that there would be a lawsuit should something happen to a child. In July 2001, the National Association of Schoolmasters and Union of Women Teachers (NASUWT) announced that it is advising its members to refuse to accompany school trips because of the increased risk of litigation. Ask any school the reason why they do not offer certain types of activity and outing and it is unlikely to be because they are too dangerous or not beneficial for their pupils. The most likely explanation given will be 'for legal reasons'. The problem with the legal route in such cases is that the experiences of one individual or small group can determine the services available to all. The claim of one parent, for example, against the local authority providing playgrounds can close the facilities to everyone, not because they are necessarily unsafe but because the authority wants to avoid the risk of litigation.

Increasingly, through this pattern of organizations trying to reduce the risk of being sued – no matter how remote – choices are being made for us about what we should and should not do. Contraceptive choices for women, for example, are now determined in some measure by the degree of litigation against them rather than what most women find convenient. The danger with compensation claims is that they are focused on the predicament of one or a few individuals and the consequences of the individual claims are not taken into account. We probably could benefit from a broader social perspective on how many hip operations would be possible with the sums paid out in compensation or how many roads could be built with the payments made by local authorities to slip and trip claims, for example.

◆ ● ● CONCLUSION: WHY COMPENSATION CLAIMING ● ● IS NOT SOCIAL JUSTICE

The American legal system has its roots in a grand scheme of 1960s social engineering, when a group of judges embarked upon the creation of a system to compensate effectively for the lack of a welfare state. Through the courts, and from the coffers of the corporations, it was envisaged that the poor could receive (financial) justice in the absence of a comprehensive welfare system. In Britain, this David and Goliath conception of litigation was imported from the USA in the 1980s, by personal injury lawyers and campaigners, in the context of the rise of victims' rights and increasing hostility to large corporations. It is now a more mainstream assumption that the legal system can be used as an instrument for social justice.

As a way to allocate resources to injury victims, the legal system is very costly (especially because of the number of intermediaries involved), time consuming and arbitrary. It is also hardly surprising that this 'social justice' project has been a conspicuous failure, either as a means of gaining justice or of redistributing wealth. A simple measure of its iniquities is the fact that personal injury lawyers are highly selective in the cases they take on. Many people are not eligible for compensation and many cases are seen as too high risk relative to the rewards available for the lawyers. It would be better to improve welfare to deal with the losses people suffer irrespective of whether it is through negligence or unavoidable accident. All in all, litigiousness is a very blunt instrument.

Some lawyers, when challenged about their claims of social justice, are forced to accept that the role and capability of the legal system is not to redistribute wealth and power in society – it can only deal with individual cases. But, they argue, in the absence of good welfare service provision for people who need medical care or to take time off work, the legal system is just stepping in to fill a void, never mind how patchily it does it. There are problems with this argument.

If we continue to allow compensation claiming to develop into the dominant way of getting what you need, we are unlikely to find anything better or fairer. Compensation claiming is damaging the very relationships and sense of responsibility that are essential to coming up with social and political solutions to problems. How is this so? Compensation culture is a barrier to better sources of 'social justice' because individuals make their own individual claims. It is not *social* at all. Those who claim do not have to take into account anyone else's predicament or try to change anything about how society works other than for themselves. From an individual vantage point, one's experience of life often looks unfair. For example, if you were unlucky enough to be the victim of a side impact collision in your car, you may feel aggrieved to discover that the motor manufacturer of your car had considered and rejected measures to reinforce its sides (as indeed many manufacturers have done). Such measures would undoubtedly have offered better protection in your particular collision. You may feel inclined to sue. However, by far the greatest number of collisions are frontal impact, when the sides are best not reinforced so that the impact's force can be distributed away from a car's occupants. It is hard to see that bigger picture from a hospital bed. It is even harder when you live in a society that promotes the idea that injury is your best form of entitlement to resources.

The most creative and successful ways of ensuring that society is efficient, fair and able to benefit the largest possible number is to have decisions made at a social or political level. A motor company makes decisions to give it greatest business success, but this still takes in more of the social picture than do claims by injured individuals. Needs have to be prioritized. There is not a transport system anywhere that carries no risk of accident. We have to prioritize the social need for transport above concern about the unfortunate individual who gets injured.

Unfortunately, because political leaders and service providers are becoming scared of suggesting that some people's problems do not merit changing the way we do things (withdrawing a play service because of a chance accident, for example), the ability to decide what is best for society as a whole is already being eroded. The possibility of a just society is weakened even more by the promotion of individual claims and using the law to bully for individual resources, instead of engaging with the broader social needs and consequences. The rise of litigiousness and liability has occurred precisely at a time when people are unwilling to engage with institutions in any meaningful way. The promotion of new claims and the expansion of liability are just catching on the coat tails of broader social disengagement; it is symptomatic of powerlessness. It is because of this context of individuation that I think we need to be suspicious about the idea that we are witnessing an expansion of social justice, that David is being given the opportunity to conquer Goliath. Litigiousness can be no more than a highly individuated response to social injustice. In fact, suggesting that compensation claiming contributes to social justice is a bit like saying that doing the lottery contributes to social equality! Furthermore, it is belittling, rather than empowering to conduct our relationships with reference to legal duties and threats. It is our ability to take responsibility for ourselves and for the consequences of our own actions that empowers us – not charters or lawyers.

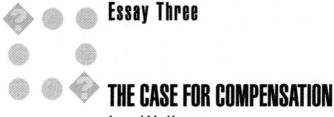

Essay Three

THE CASE FOR COMPENSATION
Ian Walker

Let me suggest a situation to you. You leave work this evening and are walking down the pavement towards the bus stop or station to catch your transport home. It is a fine evening and you are looking forward to returning home. Suddenly, and without warning, a motorcar that has mounted the pavement at speed strikes you violently from behind and you are knocked flying by the front of the vehicle and collide with an adjacent lamppost. You sustain fractures to both legs requiring surgery and you are in hospital for ten days and suffer an unimaginable amount of pain.

After some months' convalescence it becomes clear that your legs are permanently deformed because of the seriousness of the fractures and you will never again be able to walk without pain, or without a limp. It is certain that as the years progress you will develop arthritis requiring further operations. Unfortunately, your job requires a great deal of walking and standing and you are never going to be fully recovered enough to do that job. Your employers do the best they can and find a sedentary job for you but at considerably less pay. You are finding it difficult to make ends meet on your new reduced salary. At the time of the accident you were about to be promoted to a managerial position which would have involved increased status and a lot more money.

All of this happened to you because the driver of the car that hit you had been drinking to excess. He was speeding along the road and, because he was not paying proper attention, failed to notice that the queue of traffic in front of him had slowed to a halt. He realized this at the last moment and swerved to avoid colliding with the stationary vehicle in front, mounting the pavement and hitting you. This is a pretty typical story that those of us who represent injured accident victims hear every day of the week.

BRINGING A CLAIM

Put yourself for a moment in the situation I have just described. I suggest to you that you would not hesitate to consult a solicitor, to bring a claim for damages against the motorist who hit you. You would be in no doubt at all that the accident had resulted from his carelessness, or negligence, and you would be seeking compensation for the terrible injuries that had been done to you and to compensate you for your loss of career, loss of earnings and so forth.

Can you actually imagine a situation in which you would not decide to make such a claim? Strange as it may seem there are many who, on hearing of your decision to claim damages, would say that you were now part of the 'compensation culture' in society. They would say that misfortune is potentially visited upon any one of us on a daily basis and that we really should not rush to lawyers every time something unpleasant happens to us. They say that we ought to accept misfortune as part of the hazards of everyday living and make the best of what might be an appalling situation. Recently a leading motoring writer opined in the columns of the *Sunday Times* that it is the most human of characteristics to make a mistake and that people should not be sued if they make a mistake regardless of the consequences on innocent parties.

The reality is that the debate has become distorted by what are seen as 'fringe' actions for damages and I will go on to consider these in a moment. However, I venture to suggest that those people who are in the forefront of the clamour against a 'blame culture' and a 'compensation-driven society' would not hesitate to bring a claim for damages if they found themselves in the terrible and distressing circumstances that I have just described. The level of hypocrisy in this debate has now really got out of all proportion.

 **THE COMMON LAW**

Why, therefore, is there any debate at all? Why are some commentators seeking to suggest that the common law, which has protected the rights of individuals for hundreds of years, is suddenly at the heart of an alleged change in society which is deemed to be wholly harmful to that society and which should be discouraged?

The common law exists to ensure that we all are held accountable for our actions. The common law accepts that from time to time mishaps do occur and that this is part of the normal fabric of society. The common law demands no more than at all times we do what is reasonable to protect others from coming to harm as the result of our actions. I suggest that this is a test with which no one could seriously disagree as being for the benefit of society. To say otherwise would mean that we had freedom to act as we wished and that if we injured someone as the result of failing to take proper care we would not be held accountable at all.

We could drive along the streets as we wished because it would not matter whether we hit other cars or pedestrians because we could not be held accountable if we caused them harm. We could allow our houses to become appallingly dangerous death traps and it would not matter if visitors to our homes were injured when they fell through a floorboard that we had neglected to repair or were hit by a tile from the roof that fell on them because we could not be bothered, once we had realized that it was loose, to have it fixed.

I believe that, in respect of 95 per cent of the claims that are brought by those who are injured as a result of a negligently caused accident, the public at large would have no lack of support for the injured person and would take the view that it was wholly right and proper that they should be properly compensated for the injuries that they received through no fault of their own, but through the complete lack of care of somebody else.

It is vitally important to remember that claims will not succeed unless negligence can be proved and personal injury lawyers on a daily basis are telling clients that they cannot proceed with their claim because negligence cannot be proved or because the English law does not allow a remedy. To suggest, as many have, that we happily spend our time bringing fanciful claims is a million miles from the truth.

 ## CLINICAL NEGLIGENCE CLAIMS

One area that is causing great concern is the cost of actions for medical negligence as the result of injuries caused by negligent doctors, surgeons and the like. It is said that the level of claims has now got to such a high point that the NHS simply cannot afford to meet them and that the financial strain is causing resources to be withheld from elsewhere within the NHS. It is said that doctors are more likely to practise 'defensive medicine' because they will be worried about being sued if they get the treatment wrong. Let us look at the reality of the situation.

The burden of proof in bringing a clinical negligence claim is extremely high. In order to succeed against a medical practitioner it is necessary to prove not just that the treatment was wrong, but also that 'no respectable body of opinion within the medical profession would have agreed that the treatment was correct or carried out correctly'. In other words, if you have a situation where the surgeon admits that the treatment went wrong, but can produce a number of eminent colleagues who would have done exactly the same in his or her position, the claim will fail. Whether or not one agrees with that as being a correct way for these claims to proceed may be debatable, but it is how the law works at the moment. The result is that it is extremely difficult, except in the clearest cut cases, to prove negligence in a clinical negligence setting.

However, that is not really the point. There are thousands of claims brought every year where the National Health Trust concerned, or the individual clinician concerned, admits that they were negligent and where compensation is payable as a result. The doctors actually agree that they failed in their proper duty to their patient. They have agreed that they did not do everything that was reasonable and that the standard of care that they visited upon their patient was woefully less than the patient was entitled to receive. Claims are not paid by the National Health Service unless negligence is, overtly or covertly, agreed.

Why should it be suggested that these innocent victims of a doctor's negligence should be in any different a position from the road accident victim whose plight was set out at the start of this essay? Why should doctors have any immunity from being sued if they are so negligent that the treatment harms their patient in circumstances where there should have been a recovery? How on earth can it be argued that if the doctor makes a negligent mistake he or she should not be required to compensate a victim who is harmed as a result? The proposition is, frankly, ludicrous.

If the National Health Service wants to cut the cost of claims there is a very simple remedy: stop the negligent treatment in the first place. If you do not cut off the wrong leg in an operation then the patient will have no grounds to sue you. If you do not inject a massive overdose of a dangerous drug into a child's spine, he will not be able to bring a claim against you. If you do not deprive a baby of oxygen during the birth process, causing him or her to be born with cerebral palsy, then no one is going to consult lawyers to bring a claim against you. The answer is that simple. If you get the treatment right, if you take proper care, if you do not act negligently then people will not sue you.

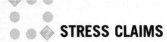

STRESS CLAIMS

Let us look at another area that is causing concern: the question of occupational stress. It is said that the claims brought by those who have been forced into a nervous breakdown by their employers are ridiculous and should be stopped. It is said in particular that those who joined the emergency services know full well what they are getting into and should not be entitled to sue anyway if the stress of the job proves too much for them. Again, a look at the facts is probably in order here.

The law requires that an employer takes reasonable care to protect his or her employee from coming to harm. As a result of a European directive we have a very widespread and complex framework of regulations in this country which ensure that employers take proper care of their employees. In most cases the test is again one of reasonableness; if an employer does all that is reasonable to protect his employee from harm then it is highly unlikely that any claim will succeed even where very serious injuries occur through an industrial accident.

It is exactly the same law that applies to broken legs in a steelworks that applies to a broken psyche in an office situation. An employer has a duty to ensure that an employee is not harmed by their work and that includes ensuring that they are protected from harm from stress. This protection may in many cases mean the removal of the employee from a particular occupation because they do not have the requisite strength and personality to deal with the stress of a particular job. The reality is, however, that those cases in this area which have succeeded have been where the employer has been put on specific notice that an employee is suffering from levels of stress, because of his or her work, which are likely to harm him or her and who has done absolutely nothing about it. Those claims have succeeded where the employer has been shown in the court that he or she really could not care less about the welfare of the employee and did nothing at all to respond to the clear signals that were being given that this individual was likely to have a nervous breakdown unless something was done about their work situation.

In practice very few of these claims have succeeded because, for all sorts of technical reasons, they are very difficult to pursue. However, how can it be argued that it is all right for an employer to have to protect an employee from the danger of physical harm, but that the employer can be completely free to inflict psychological harm without being held to account? Again the proposition is ridiculous.

 **OTHER CLAIMS**

Those who have responsibility for our children seemingly get extremely upset where a child has sued a school for failing properly to take care of one individual. Again it must be stressed that these cases are extremely rare and, again for technical reasons, very difficult to pursue. But consider this proposition. You have a child who has learning difficulties. As a parent you are not an expert of this because you do not have the training or the experience or the knowledge properly to diagnose why it is that your child appears to have difficulty studying. The teachers at the school, however, do have such knowledge and experience and ought to have spotted that the child is dyslexic. Because they failed to take proper care of that child, because they failed to notice that dyslexia might have been a problem, and because they failed to ensure that proper tests were carried out to see if dyslexia was the problem, the child's education was effectively ruined and the child's future irrevocably damaged. No one is saying here that every child who has a difficult education should sue the school and no one has sought ever to suggest this. Again what is said here is that if individuals have experience and knowledge, and are in a position of authority, they have to make sure that they use that experience and knowledge carefully. If their conduct clearly exhibits that they could not have cared less then it is surely right and proper that compensation should be paid to those whom their indifference has harmed.

One could go on listing the various situations where the common law has come under attack. The reality is that individual pressure groups have focused on one or two claims which have been brought at the extreme edge of the common law, many of which have failed in the process and have condemned the whole common law system outright.

DAMAGES

It is often assumed that those who succeed in obtaining damages receive a great windfall. This is certainly the image projected by the so-called 'claims farmers' who advertise on our television screens. The reality is that the level of damages paid by the English courts cannot by any stretch of the imagination be called generous.

In most serious cases the damages for the actual injury is a relatively small percentage of the total award. Most claims reach large figures because the damages include awards for loss or earnings, actual financial losses flowing from the accident, medical costs and so forth. In other words, the victim is being paid back sums that they have actually lost because of their injuries or sums that they will have to pay in the future. Hardly a windfall there.

Even when one considers damages for injuries suffered, the sums often do not equate with what ordinary members of the public would feel reasonable. For example, a young woman who suffers a leg amputation just below the knee could expect to be awarded about £50,000. A young man who breaks his back and will be paralysed from the chest down and in a wheelchair, for the rest of his life can expect only about £130,000. An injury causing a serious fracture to the wrist, as a result of which the wrist has to be surgically permanently stiffened, gets £24,000.

The first two cases will, of course, receive much higher sums in practice, as other items will be added on – loss of wages, nursing care, prostheses and so forth. In reality, no one would ever believe that the injury they suffered and the effect that it had on their life is worth the money. Claims are being brought at a higher level today than 20 years ago not because people are financially motivated, but for many other reasons.

THE 'COMPENSATION CULTURE'

The truth of the matter is that more personal injury claims have been brought not because we have this so-called 'compensation culture' but for a number of different and interlinked reasons. We are, as a society, much more conscious of our legal and moral rights than we were, say, 50 years ago and are less likely to treat infringement of those rights, real or perceived, without challenge. I suggest that this is, in fact, a healthy thing for society and provides a natural and effective check against oppressive government and oppressive corporate conduct.

We are better educated and better informed than previous generations, particularly through the growth of effective broadcast and print media, and we are therefore aware about matters which are going on which many years ago might otherwise have been covered up. This means that litigation for defective drug products, for example, is much more likely now than it would have been 50 years ago.

We do not have the close family network that our grandparents' generation had and therefore have not yet developed strategies to enable us to cope with adversity. This means that we are more likely to be more psychologically affected by misfortune than would have been the case years ago. Whether or not one likes that situation it is a fact.

Access to lawyers has been made easier than ever before. People are aware that it is possible to get free advice from an experienced lawyer to discuss their problems whereas previously the thought of going to a solicitor would have filled most people with terror. The growth of trade union legal schemes and legal fees insurance has contributed to this as well.

Often, it is only through litigation that the truth behind an accident can be discovered. Those who have caused accidents may be tempted to cover up the truth, but through the litigation process all secrets are laid bare. The medical profession is now much more open about explaining why things went wrong at an operation, knowing that if they do not explain litigation will force them to.

All this is, in fact, a positive thing for society. It is a good thing that injured employees are able easily to bring claims against their negligent employer; these claims highlight dangerous industrial practices and have proved to be effective in promoting legislation for a safer working environment. It is a positive thing that manufacturers of harmful and dangerous productions are held up to account for their actions. It is only through the medium of civil claims that dangerous safety issues in public transportation, for example, are highlighted; the grouping together of victims and their lawyers to form a united front against the perpetrators of rail disasters may ensure a safer network in the future. The ability of innocent victims of dangerous drivers to receive proper compensation to help them rebuild their lives is an essential part of the caring and supportive fabric of society.

People do not rush off to lawyers every time misfortune befalls them. They rush off to lawyers every time their rights are infringed. They hurry to lawyers every time they have been needlessly injured by the negligent acts of others. They contact lawyers when employers who care nothing for safety have maimed them. The common law system has protected innocent members of the public for centuries; those who would challenge its continued existence do so at the risk of abolishing the rights of individuals to go about their daily business without fear of being needlessly harmed.

Essay Four

THE COMPENSATION CULTURE: A NEW LEGAL PATERNALISM?
Daniel Lloyd

Claims for compensation in the law of negligence have always been made but today legal claims are being brought which could not have succeeded in the past. In the last ten years or so, many new types of harm have been discovered, for which compensation can be claimed. Many new classes of defendants have also been created against whom damages can be awarded. Today the law recognizes claims for compensation that once would have been dismissed as spurious or without merit. Instead, the law now condones behaviour that in a different era would have been considered irresponsible and reckless.

In this essay I first briefly survey the types of new claim now being made, claims that would not have been countenanced by the law in the past. In the second part I look at some of the legal problems that this pattern of claiming has created. My argument is that the law has not survived unscathed and that much of the law's internal coherence has been lost, as it has sought to accommodate the new types of claim being made. I will then look at how the law has attempted to address these issues and in the final part advance my own ideas as to how the problem of the compensation culture might be better addressed.

◆ ● ●
● ●
● ● ◆ **THE COMPENSATION CULTURE**

The law of negligence no longer represents a haven of certainty and body of learning that can be trusted in determining who should be liable (if anyone) for harms suffered. Today, for plaintiff lawyers, the law of tort is a wonderful place full of fantasy and adventure where the law is a laboratory for experimentation with new kinds of claim. For lawyers defending public authorities and large companies the law of negligence is now a strange, nightmarish world where the defendant is always liable. Let's look at some recent examples.

In a group action suit, 350 soldiers are suing the Ministry of Defence (MOD) for suffering post traumatic stress disorder. They are claiming compensation on the basis that the MOD failed to prepare them for the full horror of war. They say they were poorly trained, exposed to unnecessary danger and afterwards their conditions were not recognized or treated. Members of the group have served in recent conflicts such as Bosnia, the Gulf War, the Falklands or Northern Ireland, and are claiming compensation for the post traumatic stress disorder they have suffered since (*Daily Telegraph*, 3 April 2001).

This group action is the latest in a long line of cases brought against the MOD. The first attempt by soldiers to sue the MOD for providing a dangerous working environment was *Mulcahy v MOD* (1996). Mulcahy fought in the Gulf War in an artillery unit. He suffered damage to his hearing because the guns were very loud. He sued the MOD. His claim was thrown out but only once it had reached the court of appeal. The current group action for post-traumatic stress potentially represents a serious financial problem for the MOD. In 1994 they settled a claim for post-traumatic stress disorder from a former Scots Guardsman, who had fought in the Falklands, for £100,000. Settling the claims in the group action suit for a similar amount of compensation could leave the MOD facing a bill of up to £50 million. At the time of writing, the case was yet to come to court, but whatever the outcome, it is significant that it has been brought at all. That it has, suggests that past assumptions about what it means voluntarily to take on the responsibility that comes with becoming a member of the armed forces have been undermined. In this type of claim the law is being invited to disregard the question of personal responsibility and, instead, blame the MOD for the fact that involvement in war can damage one's health.

Claims that would not have been countenanced in the past are not confined to those brought by the armed services. Civilians, too, are bringing actions that represent a new development. In 2000, Mrs Jean Gratton sued the travel company, Airtours, after a coconut dropped onto her chest while she was reclining under a palm tree in the Dominican Republic. She alleged the accident could have been fatal. Airtours settled the claim for £1,700 (BBC News Online, 8 May 2000). In 1999 a woman sued Durex for £120,000 when she became pregnant after the condom her partner was using broke. The claim was ultimately dismissed but not until large sums of public money in the form of legal aid had been paid to her lawyers. In another case, a woman picked up £195,000 after her employer 'wrecked her job prospects' by refusing to supply a reference.

Until at least 20 years ago, these claims would have failed. They would have been dismissed by the courts on the basis that they disclosed no cause of action, or because the type of harm for which compensation was being sought was not deemed worthy of compensation by the law. Of course, many of the cases referred to have proved to be unpleasant experiences for the individuals involved and few would want to put themselves in their position. But in the past the law would have deemed these individuals to be capable of bearing the loss suffered and, moreover, the law would have expected them to be capable of picking up the pieces and carrying on without financial compensation. In contrast, today the law of negligence seems more and more to consider the plaintiff incapable of self-help and judges that they, therefore, should be compensated accordingly. This paternalism is new to the law and represents a potentially serious problem.

If the law of negligence really does assume now that individuals are to be considered helpless and incapable of taking responsibility for their own lives, then it will be forced to intervene in many situations which in the past have remained outside the law's domain. The danger for the law in this scenario is that it ends up promising solutions to problems that have no legal answer and in the process raises people's expectations of what the law can achieve. Not only does the law risk its credibility in this outcome, it also further risks its own conceptual coherence as it bends and adapts to the messiness of everyday life. Many would say that this would be a good thing and that the law should intervene more. To them I would say this. Going to court is often a disempowering experience in that you are allowing your fate to be determined by a set of institutions over which you have little or no control. Often the law will provide no adequate answer to the problems thrown up by everyday life. Individuals often run the risk of sinking so much of their efforts into the pursuit of a non-existent legal remedy, when their efforts might be better rewarded by trying to pick up the pieces and getting on with their lives.

The problem posed by the examples referred to here is not only that the notion of personal responsibility is being undermined. It is also that judges are now inadvertently allocating large sums of public money to victims on the basis that they need to be compensated. Whether they intend to or not, this means judges are taking on a policy role in the spending of public money. Judges are not elected, unlike local councils or members of parliament, yet their decisions can only be revoked or challenged by other unelected judges. Compare this situation to public authorities that are tightly regulated and controlled by central government in how they spend public money. A judge has arguably much greater freedom to spend public money in the manner she or he sees fit than any government body has. The law is, therefore, being forced to intervene in areas where it has traditionally feared to tread. By assuming responsibility for allocating so much public money in the form of damages the law is effectively taking upon itself a policy role. Traditionally, the law has only existed to execute policy, not make policy all of its own.

The problem of judges spending public money on compensating victims of negligence is thrown into stark relief when the amount of damages currently being claimed against the National Health Service (NHS) is considered. In January 2000 the Public Accounts Committee estimated the NHS to be facing a contingent liability of £2.8 billion. In June 2001 the National Audit Office (NAO) put that figure at a staggering £3.9 billion (*The Times*, 12 June 2001). The NAO report estimated that the rate of new claims rose by 72 per cent between 1990 and 1998 and between 1999 and 2000 10,000 new claims were received and £386 million was paid in settlements. This represents nearly four times the amount paid out in the previous year.

In many ways the judges have an unenviable responsibility in deciding how that money should be spent in compensating the victims of medical negligence. But pause for a moment and think about what these figures mean. Are doctors now more negligent than they have been in the past? Do these figures suggest that the quality of medical care now available on the NHS has seriously declined in the last ten years? Or do they indicate something else? I would argue doctors have not suddenly become incompetent. Rather the figures suggest that in the current climate the courts are much more willing to find against doctors and make large damages awards accordingly.

This approach on the part of judges has serious practical consequences. The impact of litigation on the NHS is now beginning to threaten lives. 'Serious medical conditions may be missed or misdiagnosed because the huge upsurge in legal complaints against the NHS has led to patient records, including x-rays, being locked away in solicitors' offices,' the British Medical Association has claimed (*Guardian*, 16 June 2001). A survey of doctors by the website Medix.co.uk revealed how much the culture of compensation has impacted on doctors' professional lives. The survey indicated that 71 per cent said they practised defensive medicine. More than 90 per cent thought the compensation culture could affect the NHS's viability and 42 per cent of doctors had suffered a complaint or compensation claim against them in the last three years. Ten per cent had a complaint or claim by a patient outstanding against them. The survey was commissioned by the Medical Defence Union (MDU). Dr Frances Szekely at the MDU said: 'The strength of feeling among the profession about rising litigation is clearly evident in the number of doctors who have taken the time to reply to this survey. There is no doubt that this climate is having an impact on the profession both in terms of clinical practice and morale' (BBC News Online, 8 February 2001).

Lawyers would appear to be taking their pound of flesh. In two-thirds of claims for less than £50,000 the amount claimed by the lawyers in legal costs exceeded the amount of compensation awarded. Yet despite the fact that the NHS is being milked by the legal profession, and most doctors have to operate under the constant threat of litigation, Lord Justice Woolf still recently felt compelled to say this about doctors: 'It is unwise to place any profession or other public body providing services to the public on a pedestal where their actions cannot be subject to close scrutiny. The greater the power the body has, the more important the need' (Lord Woolf, inaugural talk in January 2001 at the University College London Provost Lecture Series). With this kind of attitude on display from the country's most senior lawyer doctors may have good reason to feel aggrieved.

From this brief survey it is possible to discern a number of trends which, when combined, present the law of negligence with a series of challenges. The law is assuming more and more responsibility for individuals who are now deemed to be incapable of assuming personal responsibility. The law is thereby being called upon to intervene in many more situations than it has done in the past. In doing so it runs the risk of assuming to itself a policy role in the allocation of public resources, which in the past has only been performed by elected politicians. Furthermore, in allowing itself to intervene more widely, the law risks losing its own credibility as false hopes are raised and then dashed upon the altar of legal expectation. The new legal paternalism which is being created by these developments has already wrought in its name a number of changes to the law of negligence. The principles of the law of negligence that were once relatively unproblematic in their application now give rise to findings and awards that would be anathema to practitioners from a bygone age. In the next section, I explore how the law of negligence has been stretched in such a way that many of its core principles now bear a very different meaning from the meaning once imparted into them.

STRETCHING THE LAW

In the law of negligence, liability has expanded: in what is reasonably foreseeable; in who we may be considered to be in a proximate relationship to; in the type of harm that damages can be awarded for; and in the actual amount of damages that can be awarded. The extension of liability today militates against legal recognition of personal responsibility and means the law often ends up condoning behaviour which many reasonable people would think of as reprehensible. Simultaneously, new laws have been passed that have helped to create new causes of action and new classes of plaintiffs who are able to sue. I do not intend here to produce an exhaustive analysis, merely to illustrate how some of these changes have worked out in practice.

REASONABLE FORESEEABILITY

What is reasonably foreseeable? Today the law seems to expect defendants to be legal supermen in their ability to foresee harm to others. Formally the law has not changed. The words 'reasonably foreseeable' are still used as part of the legal test to determine whether or not the defendant is at fault. What has changed is the application of this test to defendants' conduct. Defendants are now expected reasonably to foresee many types of harm and thereby foresee consequences of their actions which no reasonable person could foresee. By expanding the boundaries of reasonable forseeability in this way the law creates an indeterminate liability to an indeterminate number of people for an indeterminate amount. Hence the law undermines its ability to administer justice as it becomes more and more difficult to determine where the new boundaries of liability lie.

Take the case of Ben Smoldon who played rugby. He was paralysed in a tragic accident in a collapsed scrum while playing. He sued the referee on the basis that had the referee applied the laws of the game correctly he would have foreseen the possibility of this injury occurring to Smoldon. This places an impossible burden upon those who choose to referee. It also directly diminishes the question of personal responsibility. Playing rugby is inherently risky. Why should the referee take responsibility for those risks? In the past Smoldon's claim may well have been unsuccessful. A previous generation of judges would have, in all likelihood, allowed the defence of *volenti non fit injuria* to succeed. Under this defence you cannot claim compensation if you have voluntarily assumed the risk. The *volenti* defence today rarely succeeds, so keen is the law to be plaintiff friendly.

By finding against the referee the high court effectively said that individuals should not have to accept the consequence of their actions. That individuals should be protected even where they clearly know the risks they are entering into. This represents a new legal paternalism where the law assumes we are all incapable of taking risks and treats us accordingly. By shifting responsibility onto regulatory bodies (in this case, the Rugby Football Union, which was responsible for the referee), public authorities or companies the law is effectively denying personal responsibility.

A more recent case illustrates how far plaintiffs and plaintiff lawyers are now prepared to go in trying to stretch the boundaries of what is reasonably foreseeable. Richard Davis, 53, is suing Novartis Pharmaceuticals and his doctors. In 1989 he was diagnosed with non-malignant pituitary gland cancer. As part of his treatment he received certain drugs which he alleges the doctors who prescribed them knew to have psychological side-effects. He now claims that these drugs have caused his life to spiral out of control. Prior to his treatment he said he had only had three sexual encounters. He claims that the drugs he received turned him into a sex maniac. He claims that the drugs made him behave like a 'cross between a deranged sex maniac and a highly over-excited teenager' (*Metro*, 12 July 2001). This may be highly amusing until you realize that he is claiming £8 million in compensation from Novartis and the NHS. Richard Davis is effectively saying that the doctors who cured him of cancer should have reasonably foreseen that the drugs they used might turn him into a 'sex maniac'. The idea that Davis should be compensated is galling. The money he is claiming could be much better spent either by Novartis on developing new drugs or by the NHS on providing better healthcare.

It is only with the expansion of what the law considers to be reasonably forseeable that these kinds of claim can now be brought. The law used to place a premium on personal responsibility and assume that individuals were capable of taking risks and accepting the consequences. The law no longer places such a high value on personal responsibility. As a result the law has got itself into a mess. With every new type of claim that succeeds the law takes another step towards the land of indeterminate liability. With every new case where the law fails to recognize the importance of personal responsibility it stores up new problems for itself in the future.

CREATING NEW KINDS OF HARM THAT ARE ACTIONABLE

For what kind of harm can you claim compensation in law? The only limit would appear to be how good your imagination is. All types of physical harm can be claimed for. Mental harm can now also be claimed for even where it is not related to any other physical injury. This is a new and recent development that has only occurred in the last decade. By allowing claims for mental harm to be compensated the law of negligence has effectively opened up a whole new vista of liability.

As discussed earlier, a claim is being brought against the MOD for post-traumatic stress by former soldiers. In another area, education, new types of claim are now being brought for mental harm. In one case children who failed to pass their GCSE exams were awarded legal aid to sue the local education authority (LEA). They claimed that the LEA failed to give them an adequate education (*The Times*, 2 December 1996). They were ultimately unsuccessful but they were still entitled to public money to bring the claim.

In the field of health, claims are now being made for mental harm. In one case Lincolnshire Health Authority agreed to pay £500,000 in compensation to the families of the children killed by nurse Beverley Allitt. They claimed for post-traumatic stress. In law this used not to be recoverable as the relatives were not present at the scene of the murders. Despite this and the fact that relatives of the victims had already been compensated by Lincolnshire Health Authority, the health authority still settled for £500,000. It was a groundbreaking settlement that has paved the way for many more claims since, where the only harm suffered is post-traumatic stress (*The Times*, 28 November 1996). In another good example of dreaming up harm plaintiffs tried it on with Tameside and Glossop Health Authority. The health authority discovered that one of its health workers was HIV positive. It wrote to the 900 affected patients offering tests. All 900 were found to be clear of any HIV infection. However, 114 of them decided to sue Tameside for anxiety and shock. Their claim was successful until it reached the court of appeal where the claim was dismissed.

In another ongoing Scottish case, *King v Bristow Helicopters*, the boundaries formerly restricting claims based solely on post-traumatic stress disorder are being further tested. The claimant in this case was the passenger on a helicopter chartered by the defendant. In bringing the claim the claimant did not set out to prove that the psychological harm suffered was consequent upon suffering any physical damage (in fact it is not clear from the law report whether or not there was even an accident). When judging the case, in July 2000, the Scottish Court of Session Inner House held that 'the words "any other bodily injury" in Article 17 of the Warsaw Convention, as applied by the *Carriage by Air Act 1961*, permitted the recovery of damages for both physical and psychiatric injury suffered by an aircraft passenger' (*The Times*, Law Report, 18 September 2001). At the time of writing an appeal was pending to the House of Lords that was due to be heard in November 2001. This case has potentially serious consequences in extending the liability that airlines are already exposed to. But the case may have wider implications if it further increases the number of situations in which a claim based solely on post-traumatic stress disorder may succeed.

There have been numerous cases involving teachers, nurses, policemen and members of the armed forces claiming successfully for stress as a result of their work. In the past the law would not compensate victims who suffered only stress and other psychological conditions. The law recognized that compensating for this type of harm was inherently risky as it meant assuming responsibility for mental health and there were good policy reasons for not compensating for this type of harm. If the law does compensate for this type of harm then does that mean that nurses should be compensated every time they treat a particularly horrific injury, or that the police should be compensated every time they deal with a riot (as they are now claiming for in relation to the riots in Bradford of July 2001)? By going down this road the law is effectively assuming responsibility for individuals' mental health. The law should not be used as an instrument to relieve people of their stress by allocating blame to someone else. In doing so it once again militates against individuals taking responsibility for their own lives and encourages individuals instead to believe that someone else is always to blame for their emotional state.

INCREASING THE NUMBER OF POTENTIAL DEFENDANTS

Laws are frequently passed that inadvertently create many new potential defendants. In the recent past there are two good illustrations. The 1987 Crown Proceedings Act introduced what appeared to be a relatively minor change in the law, allowing members of the armed forces to sue government employees for damages in negligence for the first time. The MOD is now facing the consequences of this legislative change. The group action currently being brought against the MOD referred to at the start of this essay would not have been possible without this change in the law. The claim is for post-traumatic stress. The damages claimed could run into hundreds of millions of pounds. Who in 1987 could have possibly foreseen this outcome?

Another recent example is the 1992 Package Travel Regulations. Under this piece of legislation tour operators were made legally liable for every aspect of the holiday they provided. This has led to a number of group actions being brought against holiday operators for wrongs over which they could have no conceivable control. The most far-fetched case involved the holiday tour operator, Thomsons, who paid out £3,000 to two women who claimed they had been sexually harassed while on holiday in Tunisia. By virtue of the 1992 package regulations Thomsons was deemed liable and had to cough up. Companies such as Airtours have faced potentially ruinous class actions, involving hundred of claimants, since the implementation of the directive, often for aspects of a package holiday over which they could have had virtually no control.

Many laws passed may have potentially unforeseen side-effects, creating new classes of claimants and defendants. The 1999 Contracts (Rights of Third Parties) Act, although a law affecting contractual liabilities, could for example facilitate many thousands of claims for compensation being brought. It gives third parties to a contract the right to sue upon it, where the contract purportedly confers benefits upon them. It has yet to be seen how creative plaintiff lawyers will use this Act. The 1982 Supply of Goods and Services Act is another good example. The Act implied into every such contract a liability in tort whereby the supplier has to perform the service with a reasonable degree of care and skill even where there is no such stipulation in the contract itself. As a result innumerable claims have been brought under the Act for negligence where there was no liability in contract, that is, where the parties themselves had not agreed beforehand to the existence of any such liability.

INCREASING THE AMOUNT OF DAMAGES AWARDED

The expansion in liability has been more than matched by an increase in the amount of damages that can be claimed. In tort, damages are awarded on the basis of restitution, according to which they should restore the plaintiff to the position he or she was in before he or she suffered harm. But the growth in the amount of damages now awarded conflicts somewhat with this principle. The amount of damages awarded has increased by a factor of between 30 and 50 times since 1968. During the same period earnings have increased by a factor of between 10 and 12 times (see P. S. Atiyah, *The Damages Lottery*, 1997, p.66). Specific legislative changes have also contributed to an increase in awards made. In employment tribunals the removal of the old cap on the amount of money that can be awarded in damages has resulted in many law firms now taking employment law seriously and pushing legal talent into the field as the stakes have been raised. At the same time employees are now able to sue for unfair dismissal after only one year of employment, instead of two years. This has also served to increase the potential number of claimants chasing increasing damages awards.

By continually increasing the amount of damages that are awarded the law is effectively storing up problems for itself in the future. It can only serve to increase the number of people willing to make claims and thereby invite the law in to adjudicate on many more areas previously seen as lying beyond the law's empire. By allowing an increase in the amount of damages awarded the law also risks its own credibility. It may lose the trust and faith that many have in the law's ability to be even handed in the administration of justice.

Over the past 20 years, senior judges have fought a rear-guard action against the growth in these new types of claim being brought but they have been largely unsuccessful. I will now turn to look at their efforts to reign in the boundaries of liability in tort and briefly examine how they have failed in their attempts.

THE EXPANSION OF NEGLIGENCE

The modern law of negligence has its genesis in the 1932 case of *Donoghue* v *Stevenson* and one very famous passage from Lord Atkin. In the following quotation Lord Atkin outlines and gives legal meaning to the core components of the law of negligence:

> The rule that you are to love your neighbour becomes in law, you must not injure your neighbour; and the lawyer's question, Who is my neighbour? receives a restricted reply. You must take reasonable care to avoid acts or omissions which you can

reasonably foresee would be likely to injure your neighbour. Who then in law is my neighbour? The answer seems to be – persons who are so closely and directly affected by my act that I ought reasonably to have them in contemplation as being so affected when I am directing my mind to the acts or omissions which are called in question.

From this comment, there would appear to be two distinct elements to the tort of negligence, reasonable foreseeability and proximity. Where both are present, subject to statutory exceptions, a generalized duty of care can be said to exist. The 'neighbourhood principle' developed by Lord Atkin, reached, in form at least, its high water mark in a case called *Anns v Merton* (1978) and in the 'Wilberforce test':

In order to establish that duty of care arises in a particular situation, it is not necessary to bring the facts of that situation within those of previous situations in which a duty of care has been held to exist. Rather the question has to be approached in two stages. First, one has to ask whether, as between the alleged wrongdoer and the person who has suffered damage there is a sufficient relationship of proximity or neighbourhood such that, in the reasonable contemplation of the former, carelessness on his part may be likely to cause damage to the latter – in which case a prima facie duty of care arises. Second, if the first question is answered affirmatively, it is necessary to consider whether there are any considerations which ought to negative, or to reduce or limit the scope of the duty or the class of person to whom it is owed or the damages to which a breach of it may give rise.

Here, Lord Wilberforce turned the neighbourhood principle into a universally applicable test for all situations.

In the 1980s the judiciary then embarked upon a systematic attempt to reign in negligence's scope of liability by decrying the principled universal approach that had been attributed to Lord Wilberforce. In doing so their first task was to undermine the 'Wilberforce test' as it became known. They managed to do this in a line of cases starting with *Peabody v Parkinson* (1984), and finishing with *Caparo v Dickman* (1990). In *Peabody v Parkinson* Lord Justice Keith found that in determining whether 'or not a duty of care was incumbent on a defendant it is material to take into consideration whether it is just and reasonable that it should be so.' In *Leigh v Alaikmon* (1986) Judge Lord Brandon stated that the Wilberforce test could not provide a 'universally applicable test of the existence and scope of a duty of care in negligence.' This attack on the expansion of negligence by the judges became more explicit in *Yuen v A-G of Hong Kong* (1987), in the judgement delivered by Lord Keith: 'Their lordships venture to think that the two stage test formulated by Lord Wilberforce for determining the existence of a duty of care in negligence has been elevated to a degree of importance greater than its merits and perhaps greater than its author intended.' In *Caparo v Dickman* the attack on the Wilberforce test was completed when their lordships found that for a duty of care to be said to exist it must be just and reasonable to impose such a duty on the defendant.

Following these cases, the test for determining the existence of a duty of care today is threefold, unlike the two-stage test in *Anns v Merton* (1978). There must be (a) foreseeability of damage, (b) sufficient proximity between the parties and (c) it must be just and reasonable to impose such a duty. However, despite this attempt to restrict the expansion of negligence, the senior judiciary has failed in its attempts to do so.

The final category 'just and reasonable' is even more flexible and open to interpretation than the legal concepts of foreseeability and proximity. It is a category devoid of legal meaning. It may be used instead by judges as the vehicle through which they develop their own interpretations of public policy to determine whether or not a duty of care should be found to exist. It was intended to be a device through which the senior judiciary could develop a very restrictive approach towards recognizing new duties of care, on the basis that new duties of care should not be recognized unless they are 'just and reasonable'. This is not the approach that has come to be applied in the lower courts. Today judges in the lower courts often find that it is 'just and reasonable' to impose many new duties of care which in the past would have not have been imposed on defendants. If this were not the case it would not be possible to explain the increase in the number of cases brought in negligence against the NHS, against sporting bodies for injuries suffered, against holiday companies for poor holidays, against education authorities and local councils for bullying and so on.

It would be wrong, however, to blame different sections of the judiciary for the current situation. They are best understood as reeds breaking in the wind. Try as best they might to hold back the floodgates of litigation, their attempts have been constantly undermined. Judges in the lower courts, in particular, have succumbed, as social attitudes have shifted towards regarding seeking compensation as a generally reasonable course of action, and as lawyers have moved to interpret what is a 'just and reasonable' reason to impose a duty of care ever more broadly. In *The Damages Lottery*, legal scholar P. S. Atiyah recognized this when he argued: 'New types of claim are constantly being recognised by the courts, especially claims for post-traumatic stress and other psychological conditions.'

How might this situation be remedied? Clearly the judges understood the problems some time ago and attempted to put in place a more restrictive legal framework that could hold in check new types of claim being recognized in law. It is equally clear that they have failed to achieve this objective. So what should be done to redress the balance within the law of negligence? If we rely on the judges to develop the law of negligence in the same direction they have done over the last ten years, the law will continue its path towards creating an indeterminate liability to an indeterminate number of people. This outcome needs to be avoided at all costs. So what might be done to remedy the situation?

CONCLUSION: SOME RECOMMENDATIONS

It is unfair to expect judges to resolve this situation without guidance from parliament. Judges are ultimately there to interpret statutes. They are not there to make up the law themselves, although inevitably they must sometimes do so in the absence of clear guidance from parliament. Their lives could be made much easier if parliament were able to offer guidance on the following:

- Parliament should address the question of what kind of harm should be compensated for. Everyone is in agreement that physical harm demands compensation. The question of mental harm is, however, much more tricky. Thus far, judges have had to decide on a case-by-case basis, by listening to expert evidence devoid of any clear guidance from statute. I would suggest that parliament investigate this issue and clearly defines what is mental harm, what kinds of mental harm should be deemed worthy of compensation (if any) and in what circumstances. By clearly legislating on this issue parliament could offer the judges direct guidance on what kinds of mental harm should be compensated in law.

- Parliament should consider the question of damages. Up until now damages have been decided on a case-by-case basis by reference to previous cases. Parliament could make the lives of judges much easier by clearly indicating to them how much money should be awarded in damages for different injuries suffered. It would also afford parliament an opportunity to decide what are appropriate levels of compensation. If parliament set damages awards towards the lower end of the scale at least this might discourage spurious class action law suits from being brought.

- Parliament should examine the concepts of reasonable forseeability and proximity, the concepts that lie at the heart of the law of negligence. These concepts are inherently vague and open to reinterpretation by successive generations of lawyers. They have rightly been given very different meanings from the meanings they had in the distant past. However, they have now been expanded to such a point that the law is being invited in to adjudicate in more and more disputes where there really is no legal answer. It is about time parliament wrestled with the question of what should be reasonably forseeable and what is sufficient proximity. Parliament is much better placed to give guidance on these questions than a lone judge sitting in court.

These suggestions would not address the compensation culture per se. But they would, if acted on, at least allow the law to regain some of its conceptual coherence. This is infinitely preferable to the legal nightmare of indeterminate liability that is now coming into existence.

AFTERWORD
Ellie Lee

Perhaps the most difficult challenge facing the contributors to this volume is that discussions about litigation in the UK are often disconnected from each other. The legal profession has pursued its own debates about the merits of 'no win, no fee' and the lifting of restrictions on solicitors advertising. Legal theorists and academics have largely concerned themselves with issues of access to the law, the demand for 'rights' and the development and application of legal principles. More popular discussion has been focused on the size and fairness of awards, with the occasional debates about whether professionals such as healthcare workers are able to do their jobs effectively if they fear litigation. Undoubtedly, there are many more discussions going on behind closed doors, in the board rooms of companies, by insurers looking to set future premiums, among professional bodies concerned about liabilities, in councils and education authorities and so on.

There have been few attempts to bring together discussions about how the law is changing, with the media-led discussions about compensation awards and debates about the politics of compensation claiming. This is perhaps why there are complaints about the legal world being arrogant and attached to arcane language and practices. It may also explain why there are such varying expectations across society about what the law can do and what compensation awards represent. But as the essays in this collection indicate, there clearly does need to be a shared discussion between academics, lawyers, policy makers and public and commercial services so that we better understand the relationship between how the tort system is used and the resources that people need.

We hope that this volume has made a start in encouraging discussion of this kind. Inevitably, the essays here have not just offered answers, but have posed a series of dilemmas which the reader may want to consider further. In response to the question 'Do we blame and claim too much?' arguments have centred on three main themes: the treatment of accident victims; the (changing) role and character of the law; and the possible social consequences of blaming and claiming behaviour. Differences of opinion that have been debated in relation to these themes can be summarized as follows.

THE TREATMENT OF ACCIDENT VICTIMS

VICTIMS NEED COMPENSATION

Instead of castigating compensation seekers and painting exaggerated pictures of a US-style suing culture, we should be promoting the right to redress and getting rid of the stigma attached to claiming. The current system of civil justice delivers compensation to only a small percentage of those injured. The legal system screens out unmeritorious claims. It also helps to ensure that the perpetrators of irresponsible behaviour, rather than innocent victims, bear the costs of the consequences.

CLAIMING IS A PROBLEM FOR BOTH PLAINTIFF AND DEFENDANT

Seeking compensation through legal claims encourages people to cast themselves as victims and constantly emphasize their injuries. This is upsetting for people going through lengthy court actions, on both sides. Limits need to be placed on the kinds of claim that can be brought.

THE MIDDLE GROUND

The current system is expensive, lengthy and satisfies a very small number of injured people. Alternatives need to be considered – either improvements in the operation or efficiency of the legal system, or better welfare provision.

This point seems to draw some agreement from all sides, but the reader might also like to consider the following:

- Should the welfare state take fuller responsibility for people who are injured? Or should everyone be covered by personal insurance so that it is possible to afford all the necessary treatment and time off following an accident? Or should there be a standard tariff for different types of injury, no matter whose fault it is?
- Is it unreasonable that much of the cost of paying compensation is accounted for by lawyers' fees? How else could people be guaranteed access to legal redress?

◆●●
● ● **THE CHANGING ROLE AND**
● ●◆ **CHARACTER OF THE LAW**

THE EXPANSION OF THE LAW IS A POSITIVE DEVELOPMENT

Supporters of the right to compensation feel that, insofar as the application of tort law has expanded, the encompassing of new kinds of claims indicates that the law is doing a better job for society than previously.

THE EXPANSION OF THE LAW IS BAD FOR SOCIETY
AND THE INDIVIDUAL

In the process of embracing psychological injury and expanding the bases on which people can bring claims, the law has abandoned the idea that people can be held responsible for their own actions or be complicit in consenting to risks. As a result, compensation awards are often at odds with the common sense view that people who drive cars, play rugby or go on adventure holidays, are complicit in some level of risk taking.

This difference of opinion raises the following issues for the law:
- If people are ignorant of risks, who should be held responsible if there is an accident?
- Should judges be given more guidance by policy makers or parliament about the kinds of claim that are acceptable and unacceptable?
- Could stricter application of the law (that is, allowing fewer cases to succeed) influence what happens in out-of-court settlements?
- Should out-of-court settlement be discouraged instead of, as presently, encouraged because it is unaccountable?

◆ ● ●
● ● **THE SOCIAL CONSEQUENCES OF**
● ● ◇ **BLAMING AND CLAIMING**

BLAMING AND CLAIMING DAMAGES THE SOCIAL FABRIC

Those who are concerned about blaming and claiming point to the
damaging effect of the *fear* of litigation as much as the *cost* of it. It is
argued that access to medical and other services is compromised
when professionals make decisions based on covering their backs
legally rather than on professional judgment. The satisfaction of
individual claims often prompts the removal of facilities and
opportunities to others, whether that is the availability of products that
the majority are happy with, or the provision of play amenities for
children. Worse still, people become suspicious and uncertain in their
dealings with one another, afraid that well-intended help or advice,
such as first aid, will lay them open to legal claims.

BLAMING AND CLAIMING IS NEUTRAL OR IMPROVES SOCIETY

In opposition it is argued that doctors, education authorities and big
companies should only be afraid of litigation if they do something
wrong. Otherwise they have nothing to fear. Indeed, it is suggested
that the threat or reality of compensation claiming will push big
companies in particular to improve their services, and make them
more accountable for their actions.

This is, perhaps, the most underdeveloped aspect of the
compensation debate. Where the consequences of compensation
claiming are making themselves felt, it is difficult to quantify them
other than through the infrequent examples of financial impact. The
popular discussion rarely goes deeply enough into the issues to make
an assessment of them:

- Should injured individuals be wary of the broader consequences of making a claim, for example, if it restricts others' access to health provision? Or is the management of these wider resource issues a policy matter?

- Would it be worthwhile to spend money and effort investigating the level of off-the-record claiming and its effects?

- Are there better ways of regulating services and behaviour than the fear of litigation?

Whatever one's view on the 'compensation culture' debate, the issues raised present more than an intellectual challenge. They present tough questions for policy makers and illustrate the importance of understanding the impact of compensation claiming in Britain – who it benefits, who it fails and whether the sum total of its consequences is desirable.

DEBATING MATTERS

Institute of Ideas
Expanding the Boundaries of Public Debate

If you have found this book interesting,
and agree that 'debating matters', you can
find out more about the Institute of Ideas
and our programme of live conferences and
debates by visiting our website
www.instituteofideas.com.
Alternatively you can email
info@instituteofideas.com
or call 020 7269 9220 to receive a full

⌐ about